RACHEL MADDOW

RACHEL MADDOW

LISA ROGAK

THOMAS DUNNE
BOOKS

NEW YORK

First published in the United States by Thomas Dunne Books, an imprint of St. Martin's Publishing Group

RACHEL MADDOW. Copyright © 2019 by Fat Pencil, LLC. All rights reserved. Printed in the United States of America. For information, address St. Martin's Publishing Group, 120 Broadway, New York, NY 10271.

www.thomasdunnebooks.com

Designed by Omar Chapa

The Library of Congress Cataloging-in-Publication Data is available upon request.

ISBN 978-1-250-29824-9 (hardcover)
ISBN 978-1-250-29825-6 (ebook)

Our books may be purchased in bulk for promotional, educational, or business use. Please contact your local bookseller or the Macmillan Corporate and Premium Sales Department at 1-800-221-7945, extension 5442, or by email at MacmillanSpecialMarkets@macmillan.com.

First Edition: January 2020

10 9 8 7 6 5 4 3 2 1

For Alex

CONTENTS

RACHEL
MADDOW

INTRODUCTION

F OR JUST ABOUT her entire life, Rachel Maddow has been hard
to miss.

Whether it was the day when she was only three years old
and nonchalantly picked up the newspaper and started sounding out the words, or when she was accepted as a Rhodes Scholar
and dyed her buzz cut bright blue to celebrate, or as a five-foot-
eleven adult who's happiest dressed in her favorite self-described
"third-grade-boy" attire of jeans, T-shirt, and sneakers, she's always stood out in one way or another.

But she's become most prominent for her intelligent banter
and lightning-fast wit, as well as her ability to convey information to others in an entertaining way, whether she's defending
her doctoral thesis, calling out a list of snow-day school closings on local radio in Massachusetts—complete with sound effects—or explaining on her TV show the most plausible reasons
why a certain president would be using Russian talking points
during a cabinet meeting.

Rachel Maddow has taken a truly unorthodox path to stardom, and she has never apologized or changed who she is to get where she is today. Indeed, in many cases—particularly concerning her sexuality—she's openly flaunted it: This is who I am, take it or leave it.

"I don't make apologies for who I am, and I don't hold back," she's said.

She considers herself to be an outsider, first and foremost, and this has shaped her philosophy and career like nothing else. "I never feel like I fit in, and that's my superpower," she admitted. "That forces me to struggle out of insecurity, which somehow results in success. I still feel like a criminal, like I've stolen some more deserving person's television show."

Her reputation for overpreparation—a rarity in the world of fast-paced cable and broadcast news—is famous throughout the industry. Even when she was guest hosting for Keith Olbermann on *Countdown*, she'd arrive at MSNBC at nine in the morning to prepare for a show that wouldn't air until eleven hours later; indeed, there are many hosts who glide into the studio an hour or two before airtime, largely leaving the sausage making to the staff. Not Rachel. "I've been in the TV game a long time, and I've never seen anyone prepare like she does," said Bill Wolff, executive producer of *The Rachel Maddow Show*.

While she loves nothing more than to impart new information—or a new twist on an old topic—to millions of viewers, she is a loner at heart and works best by herself, behind a closed door where she can have time alone to indulge her curiosity, dig for obscure facts, and write an opening monologue that is both entertaining and informative *and* provides a new spin on a well-worn headline. She's also been open about her personal struggles, including the fact that she suffers from depression.

"I am not a model of mental health," she's admitted.

And she openly acknowledges that what motivates her is the fear of failure. "It's very boring and sad, but I want to convince myself that my existence matters," she said, which is hard to fathom given the years she spent as an activist fighting for people with AIDS. "Rachel, as I knew her, has always been about making a contribution," said Cory Booker, the former mayor of Newark, New Jersey, and now the junior senator from New Jersey, who was friends with her at Stanford and Oxford. "She wanted to change the world."

"She's unique," said Matt Delzell, managing director at The Marketing Arm, a branding agency. She refuses to toe the line when it comes to any party, while remaining loyal to liberal values in the true sense of the word. "Her uniqueness and her underdog appeal draw people in, regardless of whether they agree with her opinions," he added. "She's not afraid to criticize liberals despite being a liberal."

Indeed, she relishes her role as an equal opportunity critic. "I'm interested in making fun of bad ideas, regardless of who has them," she said, adding that she has long welcomed the staunchest of conservatives onto her show, where she has been honestly curious—and eager—to hear what they have to say. "We just click," said Michael Steele, former chairperson of the Republican National Committee. "She listens. It's one of the reasons I love going on her show. And when it's all said and done, no one is angry, no one is bloody."

"I certainly don't agree with her politics at all, but she's a really nice person," said Tucker Carlson, who regularly invited Rachel onto his show, *The Situation with Tucker Carlson* [later changed to *Tucker*] between 2005 and 2008, to debate the topics of the day. "It's very hard to find people who can argue well, who can argue from principle. She's a person of principle."

She is also hugely patriotic and has been known to tear up whenever she hears "The Star-Spangled Banner" play. "I am a person who feels personally aggrieved by people who undermine our constitutional republic," she said. "I think the Fourth Amendment is personally wired into my DNA."

Despite her obvious excitement when talking about certain stories on camera, Rachel maintains that she's oddly calm, especially when working on a story that has everyone else up in arms. "I don't have an emotional reaction to the news," she said. "It's like if you're a surgeon who's removing brain tumors. While you're doing the surgery, do you feel sad for the person having gotten the tumor? No, you're working on taking care of the tumor and fixing it."

Underscoring everything is the clear fact that she respects the intelligence of her audience, which can be a hard thing to find on any network or cable show out there today. "If you assume that your audience is as interested in what you are talking about as you are, you're going to connect with your audience in a much better way," she said.

Despite these contradictions—or maybe because of them—millions love her and tune in regularly for her honesty and willingness to say what few other public figures will say, and for not hiding her glee whenever crooked, incompetent, or just plain mean people—politicians and otherwise—get caught. But even in these moments, she never belittles the scoundrels.

"Even though I can be harsh in my criticism and I can be strong in my beliefs, I try not to be mean," she said. "And I don't have a very high tolerance for other people who are cruel or personally insulting in a way that I think is meant to humiliate people."

"You'd have to be a really miserable specimen of a human being to not like her," said Keith Olbermann, who encouraged MSNBC to give Rachel her own show.

"I have always felt like my job is to chart the waters," she said. "And we are at sea."

At the same time, she has never tried to conceal her ambition; after all, she dreamed of having her TV own show for many years before it actually happened. "You reach people in television in a way that allows you to make more of an impact," she said. "If that's the game you've decided to play, you might as well try to win."

CHAPTER 1

"Who Is That Kid and Where Did She Come From?"

R<small>ACHEL</small> A<small>NNE</small> M<small>ADDOW</small> was born on April Fools' Day 1973, and almost from the very beginning, she was showing signs of the wonky but entertaining public persona she'd grow into several decades in the future.

"Rachel arrived with a real quizzical look on her face, wanting to check everything out," said her mother, Elaine Maddow, adding that her daughter was a pretty lively kid to boot.

"She was born grown-up, and she never talked baby talk," said Elaine, noting that Rachel had taught herself to read around the age of three by reading the newspaper each morning. "We [kept] saying to ourselves, Who is that kid and where did she come from?"

Which was a reasonable question, given her parents' heritage.

Elaine Gosse was born on June 16, 1941, in Newfoundland, Canada, into a conservative Catholic family where she was one of eight brothers and sisters; her father was a fisherman. "All I ever saw my mother do with eight children was work hard, so I thought, well, maybe I would just not do that," Elaine remembered. "I'd be a career lady or sail the seas or do something really different." She moved to California in 1963 to become a portfolio analyst for the financial company Dean Witter.

Robert—Rachel's father—had grown up in Arizona and Southern California and graduated from Stanford University in 1964. He was in his second year at UC Hastings College of the Law in San Francisco when he met Elaine at a party. He served in Vietnam as a captain in the Air Force between 1967 and 1972, working as an attorney and liaison between the military and various gun and weapons manufacturers. He and Elaine married in 1968, and their first child, David, was born in July 1969. When Rachel was born, he changed careers and began working for the local water authority, the East Bay Municipal Utility District.

Rachel's paternal grandfather emigrated from Russia, and though he was Jewish, he raised Rachel's father as a Protestant. Robert and Elaine—who came from a devoted Catholic family—decided to raise their future children as Catholic, and Robert actually converted to Catholicism in 1981.

Elaine became an American citizen—when she was eight months pregnant with Rachel—because she wanted to vote in local and national elections, though it could also have been because she spent the afternoons during her pregnancy with Rachel watching the Watergate hearings on TV. In fact,

Elaine marveled at her young daughter's sense of compassion. "She always seemed to be concerned about causes and people that were overlooked," said Elaine, a trait that was sparked in young Rachel when she entered kindergarten, the same year that California's Proposition 13—an amendment that reduced property values and tax rates—became law.

"I can actually remember the library hours changing because they couldn't afford to staff it anymore," said Rachel years later. That, coupled with the state's worst (to date) drought in 1977 due to record-low levels of snowpack across the state, also fostered her lifelong environmental activism, not to mention her father's work on water issues. "Growing up in a time of drought made a lasting impression on the wet cement of my very young mind," she said. "It gave me a lifelong appreciation that water is rare, fragile, and also that water is power."

"There was a lot of discussion of fairness in our house," said Elaine. Every night in the Maddow household the family would gather for dinner and grill the kids about how their days went, asking, 'What went right and what went wrong in your day?'

"We discouraged whining," she added. "If they whined, we'd say, 'Whining is not going to do a thing. Now, how are you going to take care of it?'"

When Rachel and David were young, respectively only three and seven years old, they begged their parents for a pet, but Elaine always refused; after all, she had been raised to believe animals were there to work—such as dogs who herd sheep or help with hunting trips—or to be eaten. But they kept badgering, and their parents finally gave in and brought a golden retriever home. "My brother and I were really excited for about a half an hour, then we lost interest and it became my mom's responsibility," said Rachel. "The golden retriever ate her plants and then went straight back home."

Like many kids growing up in the 1970s, young Rachel also watched her fair share of Saturday morning cartoons, but what really caught her eye—and incidentally also influenced her path—were the educational segments known as *Schoolhouse Rock!*, a series of three-minute animated shorts that aired on ABC, designed to convert dry educational topics such as science and grammar into fun learning experiences.

One of the best-known segments was "I'm Just a Bill," which explained how the legislative process works. In fact, Rachel points to *Schoolhouse Rock!* as serving as a major influence on the segments of her show where she explains complex stories in plain language but with an entertaining and often humorous twist. She still has a soft spot for them. "When I see those, I get misty," she said.

She also took careful note of how her father "watched" sports on TV—with the sound off while he listened to the radio—which would play an important role later on when she launched her radio career. "I thought, right, radio is *harder*. He's getting a higher-level audio experience from people who know you can't see the picture," she said.

Another equally important formative moment arrived in 1980 when she watched Ronald Reagan on the family's black-and-white television after the presidential election and couldn't stand the sight of the future president. "All I remember is the feeling of dislike," she said, which wasn't a surprise, because even at an early age she was becoming aware of the huge disconnect between her burgeoning social values and those that surrounded her in her hometown of Castro Valley, which she would later describe as a "very conservative, nasty little town."

But in the sea of red, Rachel's parents were centrists, Reagan Democrats, which sometimes resulted in arguments and dug-in heels on both sides, and her family acknowledges that these lively debates helped shape Rachel's debate skills later on. "Anytime we would have a disagreement, she could outtalk me and give me a run for money," Elaine says. "It got to the point where I'd have to say, 'Okay, we're not going to discuss it anymore.'"

California presented a world of dichotomies to young Rachel. On the one hand, she grew up in the Bay Area, one of the most liberal parts of the United States. On the other hand, Castro Valley was an island of red Republican values surrounded by a sea of blue, and she realized that her intellect and compassion for the underdog were at odds with the sentiments of the majority of the population in her hometown. The grown-ups in her midst would talk fondly of someplace called Orange County, a conservative bastion in Southern California. "I thought Orange

County was a very specific thing where the people would glow a different color," she said.

Her first act of rebellion occurred at a gathering of the local chapter of the White Aryan Resistance, the modern term for the Ku Klux Klan, the skinhead racists who were common in the region. The group held rallies to attract new members at Rachel's high school and put on concerts at local auditoriums.

Rachel gathered together a group of friends and put up anti-racist posters around town and asked a group of skinheads in nearby Oakland who were anti-racists to go to an upcoming concert organized by the racist skinheads. "We were just high school kids and we were afraid of them, but we asked them to please go and beat them up," she said.

She was also a hard-core punk fan, favoring the Dead Kennedys and Hüsker Dü. "My parents were horrified," she said. "I was grounded when my mom found an SST records sampler LP in my room, I think it had particularly porny cover art and she was very rattled by it. As a teenager, I thought at the time that it was probably the apex of my coolness."

Despite her taste in music, she played several instruments when she was in junior high school. "But I was terrible at all of them," she admitted. "I was best at being the conductor."

She did better at athletics, especially when she arrived at Castro Valley High School, where she dove into playing as many sports as possible: basketball, swimming, and volleyball, which she excelled at. Rachel was more than a bit obsessive about showing up for practices and competitions; she was injured regularly but pushed through games and workouts anyway.

She'd understandably developed a reputation as a jock around school—and even dreamed of pursuing the Olympics—but she knew she was destined for more than a one-dimensional life. "Sports were the thing I did in high school, but the rest of my life didn't reflect that aspect of my personality," she said.

When it came to the movies, she favored John Hughes movies, *The Breakfast Club* in particular. And while she considered herself to be a mix of the jock and the rebellious character played by Ally Sheedy, she saw herself as John Bender, played by Judd Nelson: the outsider.

One outsider she particularly respected was Jessica Mitford, an Englishwoman who grew up in an aristocratic family and denounced her background. She became a muckraker of sorts and authored *The American Way of Death*, a book that took a critical look at the funeral industry in the United States. "[The book] was uncompromising and tough, but [written] in this witty and interesting way," said Rachel. "And for her to have come from that family and take such an outsider's perspective seemed so great."

She was slowly becoming aware that she was already an outsider in another way. In the summer of 1989, between her junior and senior years of high school, Rachel volunteered at the Center for AIDS Services in nearby Oakland, pitching in where necessary by handing out food, running errands, and answering questions for clients who she inherently realized would be alive for only a short time.

As a result, she had intuited that her "tribe" was under siege even before she had admitted to herself that she was a lesbian. She said, "Growing up in the Bay Area as a gay kid defined the world in a life-or-death sort of way. There was a sense of: Look, your life is happening now, and this may be all you get."

But coming out just to herself was still a gradual process, and while Rachel had dated guys in high school, they tended to be boys she was already friends with. In one instance, she primarily went out with one guy because she loved his car, a Mustang Fastback. "Except, I didn't want to ride around in his car and be seen in it, I wanted that to be *my* car."

She actually became serious with one guy who was a marine, and they went to her senior prom together, with him in full dress uniform and Rachel resplendent in a powder-blue dress.

But something didn't feel right. "Boys weren't as thrilling to me as they were for my girlfriends, and I definitely found myself drawn more to the charming young women in my life than to the men," she said.

When she was sixteen, Rachel finally admitted to herself that she was a lesbian. "So *that's* what's going on below my chin," she realized.

"It didn't come to me in terms of 'I think I like that girl,' or 'I think I'm falling in love,' it was, 'It would make sense to me if I ended up being a gay person,'" she said, adding that once she began to consider the possibility, more of the pieces fell into place. "It came to me as an abstraction and then very quickly became a hormonal urge. My next thought was, 'But I hate softball! I can't possibly be a lesbian because the only thing I know about lesbians is they play softball and I will never.'"

But when it came to telling her parents—or any of her classmates—well, that wouldn't be in the cards for a while. After all, her parents were devoted Catholics at the time and two of her maternal aunts had even become nuns. "I knew it was going to be hard for them to accept me," she said.

"One didn't talk about those issues at that time," admitted Elaine.

Besides, since Castro Valley was very conservative, Rachel worried that if she came out, she'd face physical and emotional harm. "I knew that it was not going to be very safe," she said.

She also had another secret that she wasn't going to reveal anytime soon: several years before she wrestled with her sexuality, she experienced her first major struggle with depression. "I was a weird, depressive little kid who never really thought I'd get to be an adult," she said. "I never thought I'd reach drinking age."

The combination of the two—being gay and having cyclical depression—caused a split reaction. On the one hand, "I was worried that I was going to have a hard life," she said.

But on the other hand, once she came out to herself, she

was incredibly relieved. She also turned her sights on leaving Castro Valley. "I knew this was not a place I wanted to be a gay person in," she said.

Not only did she regard San Francisco's gay community as her ticket out to live an authentic life, she also felt compelled to help her people any way she could. "It's a galvanizing thing to know people who are dying in numbers," she said. "To see a community come together and to see people fighting for each other and forming a secular, badass army to fight for their lives against a country that doesn't care, it was very obvious to me that that's the thing that I should do."

If her parents suspected that their daughter was a lesbian, they shied away from mentioning it. Since she had dated boys, they might have rationalized any behavior in their daughter that felt contradictory. But young Rachel had a subversive streak that ran deep and needed to be aired. So in lieu of coming out to her parents, she conducted small acts of defiance.

Her favorite act of rebellion was to "relieve" the family of its vehicles. The Maddows were a Volkswagen family: her brother had a 1967 Bug and they also had a Vanagon, a precursor of the minivan that the family affectionately dubbed "the Blue Space Twinkie." One day when Rachel was in high school, driver's permit in hand, she "borrowed" the Bug, turned onto the highway, and just kept going. Thrilled to be escaping the tight confines of her family and her politically conservative town, she drove for hours. And although she was book smart, she knew zilch about cars. As she drove, she'd occasionally glance at the cluster of gauges and needles on the instrument panel and wonder what it meant when one of the needles was inching closer to the E.

She found out soon enough when the car started to lurch and suddenly stopped, giving her just enough time to pull into the breakdown lane. The car's broken, she thought.

Despite the stress of keeping two huge secrets, Rachel continued with her eye on the prize of future Olympic gold, mostly because she believed that she had invested so much time and effort that there *had* to be a payoff down the road. "Because I spent so much time doing it, [I thought] this better be building toward something," she said. Indeed, she appeared on the radar of several colleges that were scouting for athletic scholarships. But then fate intervened in the form of an injury that she could no longer power through.

One day in her senior year while playing volleyball, she hurt her shoulder so badly that a quick diagnosis revealed she needed surgery, which required a lengthy rehabilitation period. It also meant that she would have to postpone college for a year if she wanted to pursue a scholarship.

She opted against the surgery—her shoulder healed on its own, though to this day she has trouble raising her right arm above her head—and hung up her Olympic dreams. "It was a blessing in disguise," she said.

"All the energy she had put into athletics, went into her academics," said her father.

When she was accepted into Stanford University, her father's alma mater, Elaine gave away the motley accumulation of crutches that had collected during Rachel's high school athletic career.

She wasn't class valedictorian—with her 3.9 grade point average she placed third in the class—but she had approached the school board and asked to give the commencement speech, providing them with an outline of typical generic graduation boilerplate about pursuing your dreams, blah blah blah, entitled "What a Long Strange Trip It's Been."

The board signed off on it.

But she had another secret: Her final act of defiance against the town she detested was to give a different speech, one where she'd reveal the deep-seated contempt she held against the town where she'd grown up. She sat down to write the *real* speech, which had nothing to do with her original outline. Even though she was still in the closet at high school, it bugged her to no end that parents and the school were so skittish about sex education, HIV, and anything revolving around sex. Some parents and teachers even wanted to ban certain textbooks and to promote prayer in school.

On graduation day, instead of wearing a fancy dress like many of her classmates, Rachel wore a T-shirt and shorts under her gown and Birkenstocks and "old Grandpa socks" on her feet, as she called them. She stepped up to the podium and announced that instead of giving the speech the school board had approved, she was going to take a different tack and "say the things that I've truly wanted to say for the past four years."

Murmurs and nervous laughter spread across the audience as she began by challenging her classmates to become active members of their community. She pointed out that Castro Valley was regarded as a conservative community tucked into the liberal area of the Bay Area, and that the adults in her midst regularly struggled with talking about sexual matters, including saying the word "condom" out loud.

"Castro Valley has the potential to be an exciting, interesting, progressive community, but the people who dominate it today, I don't think, are ready to let that happen. To those of you that are getting full-time jobs, joining the military, or going away to college, I implore you, give something back to this town.

"We alone are the ones that have to do it. We can't leave it up to our elders anymore because tonight we become those elders."

Her speech was punctuated by gasps, laughter, and applause, though none of the assembled faculty or administration tried to boot her off the stage or end her speech early. And indeed, her classmates gave her a standing ovation at the end.

She later admitted she was hesitant and a bit terrified about actually going through with it because she was unsure of how people would react. "I was very full of myself, and I thought that I would scandalize people," she said. More important, she came away with something that would fuel the rest of her life: "[I understood] that I could actually do anything at that point."

A lightbulb went off that night. Rachel realized that she loved being in the spotlight, making people laugh, and passing along her take on current events, all mashed up in a palatable stew, while also sticking a thumb in the eye of people she felt rightfully deserved it.

She filed all that away as she prepared to enter the next phase of her life.

CHAPTER 2

Breaking Free and Coming Out

W HEN SHE SET foot on the Stanford campus on the first day of her freshman year, Rachel already had some inkling about the kinds of careers that weren't a natural fit for her, which included the sciences, business, literature, and math. Building on the volunteer work she'd done at the AIDS clinics during high school, she knew she wanted to help people, specifically those who were disenfranchised, so she chose classes that would help her learn how to do just that. It didn't take long to realize that her chosen major would fall under public policy.

Her first year turned out to be a rough one. "I was definitely one of those kids in college who did not know how to do college," she admitted. She signed up for an art course during her first semester, and the professor handed out a reading list and a reserved reading list. Rachel didn't know how that worked; she thought she could take out the reserved books and return them at will. So she checked out the entire reserved list and lugged all the books back to her dorm room, figuring she'd get to them in the next couple of weeks and that she could renew them if that didn't happen.

When she tossed the books on her bed, she didn't know that books on the reserved list were strictly for in-library use—there was typically only one copy of each title available for a class of two hundred students—for a half hour or an hour tops, and that fines were accruing by the minute. In pre-email days, college libraries typically slipped overdue notices into students' college post office boxes, so when Rachel got around to checking her mail a couple of days later, her box was filled with overdue notices in bright fluorescent colors.

"I had no idea how any of this worked," she said years later, and felt her cheeks burning when she brought the books back, certain everyone was talking about her. She ended up paying a fine of several dollars.

She lived in Paloma in a freshman dorm before she moved to Theta Chi, a fraternity whose claim to fame was a vending machine that dispensed bottles of beer. She then moved to Columbae, a dorm that served vegetarian meals and espoused "social change through non-violent action" based on Quaker values.

Rachel felt a real sense of freedom for the first time in her life, just from being away from conservative Castro Valley and out from under her parents' roof. And being on her own was intoxicating.

But she was insecure about the fact that she had gotten in at all.

"I was not expecting to get into Stanford," she admitted. "I felt like a criminal, like I had stolen some more deserving person's spot."

As it turned out, she wasn't too far off the mark: Thanks to a peek at her admissions file she discovered that she had indeed just made it into Stanford by the skin of her teeth. The chance to view her file was the result of a lawsuit against the Admissions Department. All undergraduates were allowed to examine their files for one day only, and it was there that she learned that she was the fourth-to-last student to be accepted into the class of fourteen hundred. "[Originally], I didn't make the cut, but somebody in the Admissions Department liked the combination of different things that I had done, liked my essay, and said that I maybe had leadership potential," she said.

She was disappointed to discover that Stanford wasn't the bastion of liberal values that she had expected. "Stanford was all bright eyed and bushy tailed and into in-line skating and jogging and email," she said, none of which interested her.

She was also uncomfortable whenever a fellow student took it for granted that she was straight. What was worse, she was caught totally off guard by the homophobia she encountered from fellow students and faculty. "I was frustrated by the casual antigay stuff that I saw among college freshmen," she said.

She had met another student who had recently come out as a lesbian, who came from a family of Christian fundamentalists— her father was a minister—and Rachel was impressed by her actions. If she can be out, I can be out, she thought.

She also had an ulterior motive: "I wanted to attach my face to those [homophobic] comments and see if they still wanted to say them," she said.

So in January 1991, Rachel decided to come out of the closet. First she came out to a few friends who reacted positively and wanted to know why she hadn't told them before. "I had dropped all these hints," she said. "I was waiting for somebody to ask me." She was greatly relieved, and they discussed the pros and cons of coming out publicly; her friends wholeheartedly encouraged her.

Rachel was sick with the flu at the time, but at one point she just decided to get it over with by posting flyers in the bathroom stalls of her freshman dorm. In the flyer, she broke the ice by questioning the wisdom of the First Gulf War, which had recently started, and then dove in to announce that she was a lesbian. "I wanted everyone to know at once, and also to provoke people who couldn't handle it," she said.

Her dorm mates supported her decision and cheered her on, which bolstered her resolve to live openly. "It was empowering," she said, "there was a posse of people behind me."

But she was caught off guard when she received no blowback from the antigay contingent. "It didn't lead to any soul-searching conversations with previously homophobic people the way that my seventeen-year-old mind thought that it would," she admitted.

Years later, she marveled at her chutzpah. "It was such an obnoxious thing to do," she said. "Why did I think anybody in my freshman dorm would care? I was ninety percent attitude."

Later on, she attributed that attitude to youth and arrogance. "I thought that everything I did had to make a statement, I had a confrontational mind-set," she continued. "My attitude was not to try to bring people along gently and persuade people and show people by my evident humanity their callousness, I just wanted to throw something up in people's faces."

So she took the next step. A couple of months later she decided to come out to the entire Stanford community in the most public way possible, via an article in the college newspaper, *The Stanford Daily*.

Jill McDonough, a friend whom Rachel had confided in early on, admired her courage. "Rachel made one choice when she was seventeen, and it was a domino, it made all the other choices clear," she said. "No one at Stanford was saying they were gay, and she saw that it was a lie. She decided, 'I'm not going to be a hypocrite. I'm going to have courage.'"

The only other publicly out lesbian in her class, Saydeah Howard, agreed to also come out to the entire school with her, so Rachel called up an editor at *The Stanford Daily* and asked if they were interested in the story.

After the article was published on March 4, 1991, the reaction was more positive than she had expected, though several readers assumed that Rachel and Saydeah were lovers. "She was not one of the many girls I was sleeping with," Rachel said years later when asked about the story.

Though the entire campus now knew she was gay, she hadn't mustered up the courage to tell her parents the news. As staff writer Robin Mathison put it, "Seeing no urgent need to tell them, [Rachel] said she [had] decided to wait on it."

She wanted to wait a few days; Rachel had planned to visit Castro Valley that weekend and decided she would finally tell her parents on Friday, March 8. The editor had scheduled the article to run the following week. But then the article was published a week early, on Monday, March 4, and someone clipped the story and sent it to her parents.

The fallout was immediate and intense, and Rachel doubted her decision when she realized how much she had hurt her parents. "They were in tears," she said. "They're very Catholic and were worried that I was going to go to hell and would have a hard life. But they were also upset that they had raised somebody so callous and nasty and disrespected them enough to not tell them but tell the newspaper. They didn't deserve it, and I don't blame them. I was obnoxious."

Her mother later admitted Rachel's announcement came as a shock and that she and Bob struggled with the news both "intellectually, as well as emotionally," said Elaine. "It was worrisome because of the idea she would encounter prejudice and bias in her life. Life is hard enough without having to deal with a lot of prejudices. We just wanted her to be safe."

Rachel returned to campus, and it took some time and soul-searching, but she and her parents eventually worked it out.

Once the dust had settled, Rachel resumed her saber-rattling on behalf of a wide variety of causes and movements. She joined and organized several gay and lesbian groups, focusing on the

AIDS movement and helping its victim. "I wanted to be helpful," she said. "I felt like [the AIDS movement] was a righteous thing that I had some connection to, which meant doing work in prevention and awareness." She became involved with several campus groups to promote gay and lesbian interests and AIDS education, and she helped run the on-campus Ye Olde Safer Sex Shoppe, where students could pick up condoms and contraceptives and learn how to prevent the spread of the HIV virus.

Rachel also helped out with an annual condom-rating contest during National Condom Week, and she knew that humor would help deliver her message far more effectively. "We want to make it fun and want people to see the variety that is available," she said, adding that it was not necessary to test them out for real in order to vote for their favorites. As she drew up the ballots for the contest, her humor was evident even back then as she tried to steer voters toward lesser-known brands. "They're butt-white, clinical, and smell like old tires," she said. "Why would you want to roll a rubber tire on your schlonger?" During the actual contest, she advised that students first give them a close visual examination and then pull on them, blow them up, and/or slide them onto their fingers before proceeding to real-world experiments.

Her organizing and community-gathering gene also went into overdrive. She joined the Lesbian, Gay and Bisexual Community Center at the university, signing on to help run a weekly social night for lesbian and bisexual students, which would provide them with ample social opportunities while recruiting them to help out with various other activities offered at the center.

She also helped out with protests when conservative speakers arrived for campus events. William F. Buckley Jr.'s appearance attracted hundreds of conservative students and professors, as well as citizens from the wider community, and the vast majority showed up wearing business attire and suits. Rachel gathered together a few friends from the gay and lesbian center, and they showed up at his talk holding signs that read, "Thank you for wearing a suit and tie in support of gay rights."

She also crashed an event called Conservative Coming Out Day, stole the group's sign, and changed it to "Sexually Frustrated Conservative Mud Wrestling Day."

Undoubtedly, she was the most visible out lesbian on campus, and that, combined with her involvement in the gay and lesbian organizations, meant that students who were harassed by other students, faculty, or administration because of their sexual orientation flocked to her for advice. Many, understandably, didn't want to file complaints or charges against their harassers, but foreshadowing the #MeToo movement that would arise nearly three decades later, Rachel provided a welcome and sympathetic sounding board while gently encouraging them to file complaints.

She was also harassed on at least one occasion. Not long after her coming-out story was published, Rachel was at a fraternity party and was helping a female friend who had had too much to drink. A guy at the party yelled at her, calling her a dyke, and physically attacked her before others pulled him off of her. "I was terrified," she said. "It was a mildly confrontational situation, but because he knew I was gay he used that as an excuse to escalate it into a violent situation. I had no idea what to do." Shortly after, she signed up for a self-defense class.

In the fall of 1992, she traveled to London for a term so she could study how health and public policy played out on an international stage. She found the students at the London School of Economics to be vociferous political activists, in stark contrast to her peers at Stanford. "It was integral to what they were studying and doing in school," she said, adding that she developed a real affection for London on her trip.

Rachel was also starting to exhibit the complexity that would color her views and perplex even her biggest fans later on. At Stanford, she wasn't shy about stating that she thought that people who considered themselves to be politically correct could actually be a threat to society. "A 'PC' agenda is dangerous," she said. "Nobody's allowed to say homophobic comments, so it goes unchecked." She added that people with antigay views should be able to voice them out loud in public and get it out in the open, in part so that she could learn where their opinions originated from and try to educate them.

She found that not everyone was accepting of her out status, particularly in academic circles and even in her own department. Professors and students in her public policy classes tended to lean more conservative than liberal, and as a result she found herself espousing radical views and positions in classes and seminars in order to defend her views. "It was difficult to be out as a lesbian and out without being radical," she said. "It was hard to be who I was in that kind of academic setting, but I also think that taught me how to articulate my positions clearly and argue for myself in a way that I might not have done otherwise."

Rachel spent her summers working at a variety of jobs and internships, one year at the Leonard Davis Institute of Health Economics in Philadelphia and another in Washington, D.C., working with the National Leadership Council on Health Policy Reform, a think tank that specialized in developing health public policy. They put her to work on a project that was supposed to last until she had to return to Stanford. She soon realized that another nonprofit organization in the city had finished work on a similar project a few months earlier. Her supervisor couldn't find another project for her to work on, so Rachel turned her attention to helping launch a local office for the Lesbian Avengers, a new organization founded in New York City with the aim of improving the lives of queer women nationwide, and her co-workers even pitched in to help with media contacts and outreach and press materials.

After the internship ended she returned to campus. Despite her studies and her friends, she still felt like an outsider at Stanford. Even though she had wanted to feel like an outsider in high school, she felt that she was accepted by her peers for her frequent polarizing views, when her rebukes against the administration and social mores had received knowing laughs and recognition. That wasn't the case in college. "I didn't feel very welcome at Stanford," she admitted.

"I never felt like I really fit in, so I decided that as long as I'm here, I'd like to use the incredible resources of this place to accrue some assets, to try to build something that I could use in this fight that I felt ethically and culturally to be part of."

In addition to everything else that was going on for Rachel in college, it didn't take long for class issues to rear their ugly head. Back in high school, she had always assumed she came from an upper-middle-class family, but once she arrived at Stanford and encountered fellow students who had attended some of the country's elite private schools and clearly came from extremely wealthy families, she was caught off guard. "I felt culturally alienated," she admitted.

She found her antidote in several arenas. One was her studies. "I put together coursework that would help me be the best AIDS activist around, and I wanted to get better at it," she said. "I wasn't aiming at the future because I wasn't thinking ahead. When you know people who are dying young, you don't think, What do I wanna be when I grow up?"

And she chose her courses with this in mind. "I took statistics courses because I thought I needed to be better with the statistical part of the arguments, and I took philosophy courses because that was about rigor in argumentation," she said. "I took history and politics because I wanted to understand the context of what I was doing in public policy, and I did a concentration in health policy, even though it's the most boring freaking legal policy you could possibly study."

So when it became time to declare a major at the end of her sophomore year, she looked at the wide variety of classes she had taken so far, discovered that she had the most credits in public policy, and used that to declare her major.

Her thesis topic explored how dehumanization affected AIDS patients and activists, or "how people can have a strict moral code about how other people ought to be treated and still treat people very badly," she explained.

Even though her fellow students could be indifferent or outright hostile toward her, her professors adored her. "She was a brilliant student," said Roger Noll, professor emeritus of economics at Stanford and former director of its Public Policy Program, who worked closely with Rachel. "[She was] one of those that only come around every few years or so."

"Maddow was one of the dozen best students I have taught at Stanford," said John Cogan, a professor in the Public Policy Department. "I have never met any student who has her level of commitment and dedication to public service, bar none."

The late professor Susan Okin agreed. "Rachel has a sense of purpose and strength of character that I am confident will carry her far," she said. "She has increased my faith in the next generation."

Her senior thesis won the university's Robert M. Golden Medal for Excellence in the Humanities and the Creative Arts. "I still send students to that thesis as a model," said Debra Satz, faculty director, Bowen McCoy Family Center for Ethics in Society at Stanford.

To supplement her college workload, Rachel began to volunteer with the San Francisco chapter of ACT UP, an acronym for AIDS Coalition to Unleash Power. Founded in 1987, the group regularly held demonstrations in major cities across the country. Her work with ACT UP thrilled her and she was able to put her academic knowledge to work before she graduated. Through the organization, she also became involved with a group of people who believed the same things that she did. She was finally an activist, and it was her ACT UP work that convinced her to cram in as many credits as possible so she could graduate early.

Besides, she wasn't thrilled being at Stanford; coming out had exacerbated her feeling of being an outsider in a negative way. Money was also an issue: she had amassed a significant amount of student debt, so by graduating early she could cut down on an additional year's worth of tuition and college expenses. After she came out of the closet, her relationship with her family grew tenuous, so she was forced to become as self-reliant as possible, supporting herself and paying for tuition and living expenses even though it was incredibly difficult at times. "Even as a nineteen-year-old, I decided to take care of myself as much as possible," she said.

Because of the stress, she was sometimes tempted to quit school and fling herself into activist work, but she stuck it out because she was well aware of the value of a degree from a prestigious university. "[My Stanford degree] taught me how to write and speak in defense of a position, and what could count as evidence and what couldn't," she said years later.

At Stanford she also got a firsthand glimpse at how others

would distort and misinterpret her work for years to come. "When I graduated, the head of my department stood up and thanked me for my work on women's rights, and I didn't do that at all," she said.

She graduated with a 3.8 grade point average in just over three years, and word about her prowess was already starting to spread. She won an honorable mention in the Elie Wiesel Foundation Prize in Ethics Essay Contest, a yearly essay competition, for "Identifiable Lives: AIDS and the Response to Dehumanization," which was subsequently published in *An Ethical Compass: Coming of Age in the 21st Century*, a collection of winning essays from the contest. She also won a John Gardner Public Service Fellowship, a program that would help support her while she spent her postgraduate year working for a low-paying nongovernmental organization or government job where she could focus her efforts working on AIDS policy and activism.

She already knew she wanted to live in San Francisco, so she moved to the city in 1993 and took a job at the AIDS Legal Referral Panel (ALRP) while continuing her activist work with ACT UP.

She was on her way and always attuned to spotting injustice from organizations as well as people. In the summer of 1992, she watched the Republican National Convention on TV with a few friends, in a way to help identify the enemy. One night, Pat Buchanan—a far-right Republican who had served as senior adviser to Presidents Richard Nixon, Gerald Ford, and Ronald

Reagan—gave a speech where he declared a culture war against those who didn't believe as he did, poking a God-fearing finger at everything the Left—and Rachel—held dear: environmental rights, feminism, abortion, and gay rights.

"I felt my country was declaring war on me," she admitted.

Rachel viewed his words and ideas as fuel to help carry out her own mission as an activist. She couldn't have predicted that at one point in the future, not only would she be working alongside Buchanan, but they'd be good friends.

For now, she flung herself into the world she loved, fighting for people who couldn't fight for themselves.

CHAPTER 3

Activism and Oxford

Rachel moved into a cheap apartment on Sycamore Street in the Mission District, which was dubbed "Crack Alley." She shared the place with several roommates who each paid less than $300 a month in rent.

She started working at the AIDS Legal Referral Panel, which helped people who were HIV positive with their legal needs, drafting wills and powers of attorney and fighting eviction notices. Rachel dove in headfirst, drafting public policy for the organization and helping to develop legislation and regulations to change state and federal laws and policies affecting people with the disease. "Our job was to agitate for better HIV/AIDS policies in San Francisco, in California, and in the country," she said.

"I had to learn a little of everything, so I lobbied, testified at the state legislatures, wrote position papers and reports and fact sheets, did community organizing, gave bad speeches, labored over press releases, advocated with state agencies, and generally worked my tail off."

It was a perfect fit: She was getting paid to be an activist—with the imprimatur of a well-respected nonprofit organization behind her—while also helping people who were facing life-threatening crises.

This new form of activism was a whole different ball game from standing outside at a rally and yelling and waving signs; Rachel was fast learning how important it was to be able to communicate clearly with the perceived enemy. "This job required face-to-face meetings . . . which didn't come about because I chained myself to someone's desk," she said.

Rachel also continued to volunteer with ACT UP. There were actually two ACT UP groups in San Francisco at the time: ACT UP Golden Gate focused heavily on pushing for new medical treatment options, while ACT UP San Francisco operated from more of a social justice angle. She started out with the Golden Gate group and soon realized it wasn't a good fit.

"I was way out of my league," she admitted. "I didn't have the scientific background to be able to participate." So she switched to the San Francisco group, which better suited her activist and public policy background. ACT UP San Francisco also had a Prison Issues Group, which helped lobby for prisoners with AIDS—Rachel referred to it as PIG—and she took to the cause like a duck to water.

Despite her stipend from the Gardner fellowship, she wasn't making enough money to pay her bills, so in addition to the full-time job with ALRP and her ACT UP work, she took a job as a barista at Espresso Bongo, a coffee shop in San Francisco's financial district. She worked the morning shift, which meant she rode her bike in the dark so she could get to work in time to open for the morning rush at five, since the financial markets on the West Coast opened at six A.M. Grass skirts and safari hats were not part of the uniform requirement, but she still found the whole Polynesian vibe weird, not to mention how it clashed with her regular day job. "I served quadruple nonfat lattes to people who started their work while it was still very, very dark outside," she said. "I was a very, very slow barista."

Despite its challenges, the job helped shape her future working life. "What convinced me that office life was never going to be the thing for me [was] the soul-sucking look on the people coming in to Espresso Bongo in the morning," she said. "Our most popular drink was the five-shot espresso, [which tells you something]."

At the AIDS Legal Referral Panel, Rachel quickly developed a work philosophy where she strove to be straightforward and unsentimental and focused on doing the most good in the most efficient way possible, an often impossible task at both for-profit and nonprofit organizations.

"I do not believe in the romance of the struggle, I believe in the joy of winning," she said, adding that she viewed both ALRP and ACT UP as places where she could put her nose to the grindstone and accomplish some concrete and significant work. "I think nothing attracts people to political work more than seeming like you're winning, so you need concrete victories in order to get people's attention and make them want to be part of you," she added.

"I like to get stuff done, so I worked on stuff that I could get done."

However, her pragmatic approach sometimes veered toward the confrontational. "I believe that picking fights that have an outcome is key toward keeping people motivated in fighting, though not everybody approaches these things this way," she said.

Her overloaded schedule was tough, to be sure, but what presented more of a conflict for Rachel during this period in her life was simple group dynamics, in both her paying and her volunteer AIDS work. "I'm not a very good joiner, and I was never great at being part of a larger group, so I kept finding individual parts of AIDS activism to focus on that needed to be worked on by one person. I'd bring my findings to the group and then leave," which her co-workers did not appreciate. "I don't want to be in a group of people talking about how we feel, and I don't want to have anybody try to raise my fucking consciousness. I'm just not wired that way," she admitted.

Though she loved her work, she was starting to doubt the value of working at organizations that didn't appreciate her idiosyncratic work style, and that's when fate intervened in the form of not one but two prestigious awards that would allow her to pursue her doctorate and further her study.

In 1995, Rachel received word that she had won a Marshall

Scholarship, a postgraduate award aimed at helping "intellectually distinguished young Americans [and] their country's future leaders" to study in the United Kingdom. She was thrilled and about to accept when she learned that she'd been awarded a Rhodes Scholarship, which would also bring her to the United Kingdom but would allow her to study at the University of Oxford, with tuition and living expenses fully covered for the two years it would take to earn her master's degree.

She was caught totally off guard by the news. "It was surreal," she said. "I'm overwhelmed and very surprised, but obviously very honored. There were a lot of very impressive people going for this."

She was the first Stanford graduate to be awarded both Rhodes and Marshall Scholarships in over a decade. In addition, she was among eighteen women who won Rhodes Scholarships in 1995—a record at the time—and the first out lesbian ever to be awarded the prize. She wasn't sure which one she should choose, but her friends and professors told her to pick the Rhodes. First of all, who says no to a Rhodes? All expenses incurred in the pursuit of a graduate degree are covered. But what was more important to her was the fact that if someone doesn't accept the Rhodes, it isn't conferred on another person. "But if you turn down the Marshall, somebody else will get it, and that was important to her, because one of her roommates was trying to get a Marshall at the time," said her father.

She chose the more prestigious Rhodes over the Marshall, and as she planned her move to the United Kingdom, she decided to practically shave her head, coloring the light fuzz that remained blue. "It came out purple, but I did it again to get it blue," she said.

Rachel did this to send a clear message both to her friends— to prove that she "hadn't sold out to the establishment"—and the panel of Rhodes judges. "I was very clear to the judges that I'm not going to be a politician or a lawyer or working for the government," she said. "I want to keep doing the work I'm doing, helping people with AIDS and branching out into other social justice issues."

Despite her distance from Stanford, her stance toward her conventional classmates and the university's academic structure hadn't softened any, even after a year away. "At Stanford, everyone was lobbied to work for McKinsey, so you have all these people who want to do really exciting things succumbing to consulting or law school," she said. "I'm still as repulsed by that as I ever was, it's not what I'm about."

As she prepared to leave for Oxford in 1995, she did have a few misgivings. "I was really conflicted about it at the time since I really didn't have the desire to go to grad school," she said. Plus, she wasn't particularly excited about leaving the country to pursue a graduate degree when there was so much work on AIDS activism that she could be doing in the States. But when she considered that this was a way to get a graduate education—at one of the world's most prestigious universities, no less—at no charge, she shifted her perspective. "The whole reason I [went] was to get a graduate degree for free," she said.

When she arrived in Oxford, Rachel was determined to earn her degree and return to the States as fast as possible. She had originally intended to pursue her master's degree in politics because of her bachelor's—Oxford required a master's degree for admittance to its doctoral program—but she discovered a loophole that would admit her into the doctoral program despite her lack of a master's degree: Students in the master's program were allowed to apply for transfer to the doctoral program without any limitations or even credits earned, for that matter. "So day one, I started the master's program and applied to the doctoral program, and I spent three days as a master's candidate," she said.

She was relieved, since she was never a fan of sitting in a classroom and taking classes—the doctoral program was solely research based—and Rhodes scholars weren't required to teach, as was the case at many university Ph.D. programs. So once she and her thesis adviser settled on her thesis topic—"HIV/AIDS and Health Care Reform in British and American Prisons"—she could hole up with her books for days at a time. Rachel didn't totally swear off classes, however; while at Oxford she did attend a few statistics courses so she could better understand how to interpret data and crunch the numbers in her AIDS work.

Even though she wanted to avoid a social life as much as possible, for a Rhodes Scholar it was pretty much impossible, since the expectation was that in exchange for two years of college, the administration got to strut the scholars out every so often for school-sponsored soirees.

Diana Sabot Whitney was in the same 1995 Rhodes class as Rachel, and she admitted that she was a little afraid of Rachel in the beginning. "When I first met her she had close-cropped blue hair, a thin physique, and a distinctive personality," she said. "She wore Doc Martens boots, white T-shirts, and baggy jeans with chains hanging at the belt, and had a tough-as-nails dyke persona. [But] Rachel was one of the funniest people I'd ever met, and she was often the life of Rhodes gatherings with her dry wit."

Rachel also discovered that, as had been the case at Stanford, while she was touted as the first openly gay Rhodes scholar, she wasn't exactly the only gay person in Oxford. "There have been so many closeted Rhodes scholars," she said. "That I was actually out during the application process is, sadly, a notable thing."

While Rachel did attend the required Rhodes gatherings, the rest of the time she pretty much kept to herself. "I couldn't handle student life," she admitted, so after a year of living in Oxford, she decided to move to London, about sixty miles away.

Another reason behind her move was that she just couldn't stay away from activism and helping people who sorely needed it, and the need was obviously greater in a big city such as London when compared with Oxford. Unlike a few years earlier, when she doubted her ability to work within a specific type of activism—medical and science research—because it wasn't in her wheelhouse, she had definitely grown more confident about her skills as a result of her numerous academic awards and accomplishments. So once in London, she joined a group called National AIDS Manual—today called NAM aidsmap—where she helped conduct research into the various AIDS treatment options before passing that information along to HIV-positive clients. She also spearheaded a separate organization within that group, the AIDS Treatment Project, to help develop clinical trials for new medications and promote AIDS drugs for use within the National Health Service, the U.K.-based health-care system, and helped to set up a telephone hotline, which served as a clearinghouse for patients all over the United Kingdom.

Rachel was absolutely in her element, according to Cory Booker, former mayor of Newark, New Jersey, and currently a U.S. senator from that state, who was a year behind Rachel at Stanford and overlapped with her at Oxford. They resumed their friendship in the United Kingdom, where she showed him the places she frequented in London, including a public-housing project. "She was hanging out there, it wasn't like it was a sociology project," he said. "Most Oxford kids wouldn't have even known that neighborhood existed."

Rooming with a transgender photographer she'd met, Rachel moved into a cheap apartment near the Arsenal football grounds, a rough neighborhood that provided a welcome contrast to the stuffy high-tea-and-white-glove atmosphere that permeated Oxford. She took a room on the first floor and came and went as she pleased, though she had to be careful when traveling through the neighborhood: Anyone who stood out or was different in any way could get harassed or worse. Locals knew not to go out when there was a game going on at the stadium; whether the favorite team had won or lost the latest match, a girl who looked and dressed like a boy and had blue hair was a prime target. Rachel was mugged at least once, and as a result she always belted out a tune at top volume whenever she was in transit, walking or riding her bike to work in order to deter aggressors.

Between working on her doctorate and her volunteer work, Rachel found time for an active social life, including lots of dating. "I had an amazing social life," she said. "I'm actually surprised I managed to sustain it."

She loved London, but after living there for a couple of years she was ready to return to the States. She was partly inspired by Tony Blair, who had been elected prime minister during her time there. Blair was leader of the Labour Party, and Rachel obviously admired his progressive politics. "It made me want to be back in the United States, pushing for progressive victories," she said.

Besides, she had no choice but to go back: her Rhodes Scholarship had run its course, her visa had expired, and she had run out of money. So she left the United Kingdom in 1998 and headed back to the States to finish writing her dissertation, which she acknowledged would take drastic measures.

"Writing makes me want to blow my head off," she said, adding that one of her greatest talents is putting off writing until the last possible moment, delaying the inevitable by reading, sketching out outlines, and positing endless queries about the topic that she needs to address.

"In the end, it is only shame and panic that make me write a paragraph," she admitted.

She knew the only way she'd finish her dissertation was to cloister herself in a place that would provide few distractions and where she knew she'd be miserable. "I wanted to be super unhappy and undistracted so that the only way out of my misery would be to finish that freaking dissertation so I could leave this terrible place I planted myself in and move on with my life," she said. "Otherwise, I knew that it would take me forever and that I would never get it done."

She also needed a place where she could essentially live on next to nothing, because she acknowledged that getting a job would only feed her procrastination. Two possibilities came up: A friend of her father's—a retired Air Force officer from Orange County—stepped up to the plate. "He literally offered me space in a broom closet in the office of his law firm," she said, even though that would mean moving back to a place that alternately fascinated and repelled her during her childhood. "That would be *very* unhappy making, it could work."

Her other option was a high school friend who had moved to Northampton, Massachusetts—which the TV news show *20/20* had declared to be "a lesbian mecca"—to run a bed-and-breakfast and raise dogs on the side.

Lesbian capital or not, Rachel shuddered. "I thought that sounded like the seventeenth circle of hell," she said, though when Rachel was looking for housing, the friend and her partner had already closed the inn and had both gotten full-time jobs.

"They learned that it *was* the seventeenth circle of hell," said Rachel. But they did have a huge house. "They said that I'd be miserable here, but I could live here without paying rent and finish my dissertation. So I moved in with them."

Rachel thought that living in a small town in semirural western Massachusetts had as good a chance of making her unhappy as living in Orange County would. "I don't like New England, I don't like the country, winter is starting and I don't like dogs," she said. "That sounds pretty miserable too!"

She moved into the big drafty house and settled in to finish her dissertation, fully prepared to hate it every step of the way. "We lived like monks," she remembered. "Our heating system was an open flame in one room and we had to sleep in hats."

It did indeed fit her definition of misery. But she had no way of knowing that this "miserable" time in her life would eventually provide her with the greatest rewards she'd ever experience, in both her professional and her personal lives.

CHAPTER 4

Love and Radio

Rachel had an arsenal of tricks she used to slog through the writing.

"I don't let myself pee until I've edited [a section]," she admitted. "Even if it takes three hours, I'm just going to suffer through it. I don't consciously do it, it's just the way I'm wired. I am motivated by fear of failure and I know that and so I consciously create situations large and small in which failure is a real possibility."

Though she vowed not to volunteer for any AIDS-related groups until her dissertation was finished, she just couldn't help herself. She resumed her work with ACT UP and offered up her services to the American Civil Liberties Union as well as the National Minority AIDS Council. "AIDS is the defining thing in my life. It makes me understand the world and my place in it," she said.

Even though she had shifted to being an activist from working within the various organizations, occasionally Rachel couldn't resist participating in the in-your-face kind of activism, especially if it might result in increased attention and visibility for the cause.

In June 1999, friend Paul Davis, who had met Rachel while volunteering with ACT UP, had discovered some disconcerting news about Al Gore, who had just announced that he would become a candidate in the 2000 presidential election. "We had evidence of Al Gore going against Nelson Mandela on AIDS drugs in Africa, and we planned to release [the news]," he said.

For one, Davis had discovered that when Gore was vice president, he had voted for trade policy that allowed the pharmaceutical industry to prohibit companies in developing countries—most notably throughout Africa—from manufacturing cheaper generic versions of AIDS drugs, which the U.S. companies viewed as infringing on their patents.

"People said, 'This is huge! You have to go to New Hampshire in the morning!'" So he and a few friends—including Rachel—piled into a car and headed for Manchester, where Gore was set to make an appearance in the early days of his presidential campaign.

When Gore was starting to give his talk, Rachel and her friends unfurled a sign that read, "AIDS DRUGS FOR AFRICA" and yelled, "Gore's greed kills!" Police rushed in and escorted the protesters away from the gathering but didn't arrest them. In response to reporters' questions, Gore said he would reconsider the issue before changing the subject.

As they drove back to western Massachusetts afterward, Rachel was fired up, but she wasn't any closer to finishing her dissertation. And even with free rent, she needed some cash to live on, so she started to look for an odd job or two that would buy some groceries and pay for gas for her beat-up 1983 Saab.

She applied for a job at a video store, but she wasn't hired because she wasn't a big movie buff. A couple of friends who owned a local coffee roaster put her to work doing odd jobs, hauling fifty-pound bags of coffee beans, doing repairs, and making deliveries. But her car had a tendency to break down at least twice a week—once, one of the owners had to pick her up after the car quit on a delivery—and she didn't have money to fix it.

So they asked her to install a valve on a faucet, but she put it in upside down and the pipe inside the wall burst, ruining the Sheetrock. Next, they told her to slap labels on five-pound bags of coffee, but she somehow managed to put them on upside down. "I was bad at everything," she admitted.

But they didn't give up on her. "They told me they were down to the one thing they thought I could do that I wouldn't fail at: washing buckets. I was great at it," she said.

However, she was still broke. She started working at a recycling center for a short time, but it didn't take long for her to become disillusioned. "We'd pick up carefully sorted recycling from offices, and return to the 'recycling center,' and then we'd throw everything away," she said. "At the time, it kind of just felt like we worked at a high-class dump. I'm a real liberal, but it's made me really suspicious of recycling for my whole life."

When she told a few friends that she was looking for more odd jobs on the side, they sent her to a friend who was looking for a yard boy who could do some gardening.

Rachel had occasionally held jobs where she dug up tree stumps and raked leaves, so she thought, Gardening, how hard could it be?

It was spring, April 1999, winter was relinquishing its hold on the Pioneer Valley, and she thought that working outside, digging in the dirt, would inspire her to dig into her dissertation and finish it for once and for all so she could get on with her life and get out of this hellhole.

Rachel had her doubts that her unreliable car would make it to the job in West Cummington, about twenty-five miles from Northampton, but she arrived without mishap and knocked on the door.

Susan Mikula, blond with green eyes, was an avid gardener and serious photographer who paid the bills by working part-time as a bookkeeper. She had bought the boxy 1865 house five months earlier after spending years living in a cramped apartment in Northampton. The house had been vacant for about a year, which made it more affordable. She thought she could handle the yard and gardens all by herself, but once the snow and ice receded, she realized she needed some help. So she asked some friends to recommend somebody who could pitch in.

When Susan opened the door to see a tall raggedy woman with short dark hair wearing a Boston Celtics T-shirt, time screeched to a halt.

"I fell in love. She fell in love. It was crazy," Rachel said years later, still marveling.

"It was absolutely love at first sight, bluebirds and comets and stars," she added. And even though she had experienced it before, she knew in an instant that she was now living in a completely new world.

"It was irrational and spiritual and unexpected . . . Time stopped and [I thought] Okay, my whole life is different now."

Their conversation went something like this:

"Do you know how to garden?" Susan asked.

"No, I'm awful," Rachel replied.

"Okay, so what *can* you do?"

"I can't make anything grow, but I can kill anything or carry anything dead."

"You're hired."

As it turned out, Susan was leaving for a vacation the next day, so Rachel stayed behind and hauled stumps and brush, moved rocks, and cut back the undergrowth to prepare the ground for spring planting. While she worked, her head buzzed from their encounter. She couldn't stop thinking about Susan. "When I met her, she had her initials in metal leaf on the door of her Jeep," said Rachel. "So hot. *So* hot."

When Susan returned from her vacation, Rachel presented her with a detailed report of all the trees and rocks she had hauled, handwritten on a long scrolled piece of paper. "I gardened maybe two more days and that was it," she said.

At first glance, their partnership was an unlikely one. Rachel was cerebral, measured, a loner largely estranged from her family, while Susan's creative stirrings had been evident from when she was a toddler, and she was very close to her family, who all share a great love of photography. Susan was born in New Jersey and grew up in New Hampshire, and from early childhood her parents were never without their cameras. "It is time-honored in my family and a big part of who we are," she said. In fact, her first exhibition had just been mounted the previous year at the Northampton Center for the Arts. Plus, Susan was forty-one, Rachel twenty-six, a fifteen-year age difference.

But none of it mattered.

Despite the initial fireworks, both Rachel and Susan were involved with other women at the time. "I had never had a monogamous relationship, I had never wanted to," said Rachel. But what they felt was so pure and honest and overwhelming that they quickly ended their other relationships and then proceeded to settle in.

For their first date, Susan invited Rachel to a local fishing and hunting club where the National Rifle Association was sponsoring Ladies' Day on the Range to attract more women on a regular basis; the event allowed them to try out all of the various activities that were available. Susan's sister belonged to the NRA and Susan wanted to show up for her sister and also to test Rachel.

Rachel and Susan had a blast, testing their skills with muskets, rifles, pistols, and an AR-15, an assault rifle. They even threw tomahawks and tried out the archery range.

"It turned out that Susan was really good with the shotgun

and I was really good with the AR-15," she said. In fact, she was so good that some of the other men and women at the club stopped their own activities in order to watch her.

Though she had initial misgivings about participating, Rachel was glad she did. Not only did it put her in Susan's good graces, but she also witnessed firsthand the allure of shooting sports. "Despite my gun politics, I'm perfectly happy with shooting at a gun club and then leaving the weapons there and driving home," she said. "And I think Susan's sister was given a lot of gun club credit for having brought in some newbie liberals."

While her love life was going great guns, as usual, her dissertation wasn't writing itself. And she needed to make more money than scrubbing buckets at a coffee roaster could pay.

Her housemates in the former bed-and-breakfast were working as public school teachers and had to wake up early in the morning. They listened to *Dave in the Morning* on WRNX, an FM radio station out of nearby Holyoke. One morning, host Dave Brinnel announced that Denise, the woman who read the news and served as his on-air sidekick every morning, was leaving, and to replace her they would audition promising candidates on the air, inviting anyone to apply.

Rachel's housemates dared her to audition, which was quite a stretch since not only had she never listened to any similar kind of morning zoo show but also she was more of a night owl than a morning person. "But I stayed up all night and did the on-the-phone audition," she said. "They liked me, so then I went down to the station and did an on-air audition."

Even though the idea of making a living by talking hadn't occurred to her, working on the radio held a strange appeal, not to mention it would get her away from the odd jobs that she was never any good at. The on-air newsgirl gig still paid only minimum wage, and to do it she had to wake up at three thirty in the morning, but Rachel took it in stride.

The next day, when Rachel showed up at the station, which was located in a strip mall, Brinnel thought, "Who is this fourteen-year-old boy pulling up in a pickup truck?"

During the on-air audition, Dave asked what Rachel was currently doing for work. "I said, 'I've been unloading trucks.' He said, 'From what?' And I said, 'Bigger trucks.' He said, 'You're hired.'"

As was the case when she first figured out she was a lesbian, being on the radio brought the same lightning bolt of recognition to her. "As soon as I started talking on the microphone I was like, Oh, right! This is what I'm supposed to be doing. I wish I'd figured this out before I was twenty-six."

She began the next day. Initially, she ripped and read the news from the wire and local newspapers. But as her energy and wisecracks and views started to attract a larger audience, her role in the show grew, evolving first into a kind of sidekick and foil to Dave and then morphing into more of a host where she played her own music and added her own spin to the day's headlines while giving updates about local events, weather, and traffic. But she was surprised to discover that the thing she enjoyed most was to provide her own spin on the topics of the day.

Rachel also helped to write ads and jingles for the businesses that advertised on the show. "We did one for a hot tub company called East Heaven Hot Tubs to the tune of 'Smoke on the Water,' but instead we wrote 'Soak in the Water,'" she said. Another jingle she wrote was for Cha Cha Cha, a Mexican restaurant that started serving brunches where customers were asked to follow a dress code beyond shorts and T-shirts. The verse was set to a popular Mexican tune: "It's not just for Cinco de Mayo, we make our *pico de gallo*, so put on a suit and a tie-o, 'cause every third Sunday there's brunch."

She was game for anything. Morning radio hosts often serve as guinea pigs for advertisers' services and products. From diet programs to hair salons, the rationale is that if it works for them—and they receive it for free—they'll rave about it on the air and listeners will sign up in droves. One advertiser was a local eye surgeon promoting Lasik services. Rachel volunteered for it and the surgery was performed live during her show. All was going fine until she announced, "I can smell my eyeballs burning," at which point they abruptly stopped the broadcast.

Despite her experience, she penned a testimonial for the website: "I was pleased with how quick the procedure was and how immediate the results were. Just one day after the surgery my vision was even better than it had been with my glasses."

Neither Rachel nor Dave made any secret of Rachel's sexuality. "I was the lesbian newsgirl sidekick, and part of the shtick was that I was gay and looked like a dyke, and that offended some people," she said, which engendered regular batches of hate mail.

But she shrugged off the threats and occasionally used her sexual orientation as fuel for her job, which also included conducting on-the-street interviews, making live remote appearances for promotions for advertisers, and helping to run contests where listeners could win a prize. One time the musical *Victor/Victoria* was being presented by a local theater group and the station was giving away tickets. Rachel thought it would be funny to head out onto the street with a mike to ask people if she was a man or a woman, and if they gave the correct answer, they'd win a pair of tickets. "I dressed up as confusingly as possible, in a hoodie and big baggy jeans and boots," she said.

"It sounds mean, but she loved it," said Dave.

"It was really funny," said Rachel. "Dave thought it was the funniest thing he'd ever done in his life."

While listeners were enjoying the on-air chemistry between Dave and Rachel—she made no secret of her love of a good fart joke—others took notice of her skill for explaining the news with an intellectual bent while never talking down to her audience, even an audience of one. Station co-owner Bruce Stebbins regularly engaged with Rachel off the air and marveled at her quick wit and deep grasp of the issues of the day. "She just had such a powerful intellect," he said, "and I remember thinking, 'What is she doing here?'"

On the other hand, Rachel never viewed the radio gig as anything but a fun diversion from the stress of writing—or

completely ignoring, as was more often the case—her dissertation.

"I never thought [the radio gig] was going anywhere," she
said. "I never had any ambitions to stay in the media or go further with it. I thought I would be an [activist] forever."

Working the morning drive-time shift meant that Rachel
had her days free to work on her dissertation, but again activism was a siren call too loud for her to ignore. She began to take
time off from her radio gig to travel to prisons throughout the
South to research how prisoners with HIV were treated differently from others who were incarcerated—ostensibly to help
advance her research for her dissertation—but it didn't take
long before she got caught up with helping the prisoners and
lobbying for change.

Rachel made regular trips to Alabama, Mississippi, and other
southern states where the overall policy at the time was to seg-
regate prisoners in different wings of a correctional facility
according to their HIV status. After a compulsory HIV test,
those who tested positive would be put in a special section away
from HIV-negative inmates. This presented a problem, because
positive prisoners were denied the opportunities of their
HIV-negative counterparts, which meant there was virtually
no chance of getting parole. "They couldn't take any classes,
couldn't go to chapel, or do any anger management counseling
or anything else that the parole board would want you to do in
order to shorten your sentence," Rachel explained. And even
though they needed more medical care, the prisoners who were

HIV positive tended to receive less medical care than those with negative status.

By working inside prisons, Rachel soon grew impressed with the HIV-positive inmates she met who had somehow managed to cobble together a rudimentary yet specific medical education to help their fellow inmates; essentially, they became the prison doctors in the HIV wing.

Encouraged by their efforts—which they developed on not much more than a shoestring and in a very foreboding environment—Rachel made it her mission to help them however she could while she also pushed for regulatory and legislative change with some very resistant administrators. She soon became the go-to HIV-in-prison expert for nonprofit and government groups from around the country.

As a result of her work, Rachel developed a close relationship with the American Civil Liberties Union—which fought for the rights of HIV-positive inmates all over the country—and she thought that at some point in the future she'd take a job with the ACLU after completing her doctorate.

She finessed her activism skills in a way that would resonate later on in her TV career: She learned that it was still more effective to get flies with honey than vinegar, especially when you're dealing with far-right conservatives.

"Activism is math in a way," she said. "It's figuring out what's on both sides of the equal sign and then making it come to zero. It's a very instrumental thing."

Her patient, studied approach and involved thought process

indicated even back then that she subscribed to an intricate step-by-step formula that took many disparate factors into account, while also being careful not to offend anyone who could help and networking with everyone who could possibly be of service. "Here's the thing I want to happen in the world: I want people who are dying of AIDS in prisons to be allowed to die in secure hospices instead of jails and infirmaries. But me just saying that is not enough to get that to happen. Who's the person who can make that happen? Who makes the decisions?"

If she discovered that local legislators were resistant, she broke it down in a rapid-fire logical progression: "Why won't this law change? Because the committee chairman who's responsible for this doesn't care about this as an issue? Well, what does he care about? Golf. Okay, who does he golf with? His wife? Where does she go to church? [Can we] make her pastor care about this and talk to her about this so then she'll talk to her husband who will then talk to the commissioner? All right, now we've got a hearing."

The process was exhausting, but because she respected all sides and opinions, people opened up to her, and in this fashion she was able to help change laws in some of the most conservative parts of the nation.

Even though others marveled at her skills and accomplishments in this arena, to Rachel it was pure common sense. "You need to cultivate trust among people who do not have the same aims as you but who do not differ from you," she explained. "Having opponents is one thing, but with most of the kinds of activism I worked on, we didn't have people trying to stop us from what we were doing. We just needed more people who didn't care to start caring enough that they would take a little risk to do what we wanted."

Afterward, she'd return to Massachusetts, where she'd morph back into her alter ego: a funny, brainiac radio sidekick. "I'd come home and I'd make fart jokes about the local auto dealer," she said. Compared with her AIDS work, radio "was a low-pressure environment, and really fun. Other than the hours, it was pure joy."

But there was a major change in her personal life, and Rachel felt that maybe, just maybe, it was time to grow up and finally start adulting. On Halloween in 2000—about a year and a half after they met—Rachel took the plunge and moved into Susan's house. The transition went smoothly because they had several key things in common. To start, neither one knew how to cook or had any desire to learn. "I could make macaroni and cheese from a box," said Susan. "Rachel could make toast and salsa."

They also liked the same music. "We listen to lots of what I call kind of alternative mainstream," said Susan. "To me they're mainstream because all my friends listen to them, but it's not what you hear on the radio most of the time." Their favorite artists included Cat Power, Billie Holiday, Ella Fitzgerald, Bob Dylan, and Chet Baker.

Encouraged by Susan, Rachel finally decided it was time to stop procrastinating and finish her dissertation and get her

Ph.D. so she could go on to help even more people. After a year as Dave Brinnel's sidekick, she quit her radio job—she thought her radio days were over forever—and settled down to finish her long-ignored dissertation.

CHAPTER 5

Switching Gears

R<small>ACHEL HUNKERED DOWN</small> to work, and with Susan by her side, the next year went by in a blur as she finally completed her dissertation. She returned to Oxford in the summer of 2001 to defend her thesis, and on August 15, she received word that she had been awarded a doctorate in political science from the University of Oxford.

She returned to the States to celebrate her hard-fought victory with Susan. Rachel knew that if she hadn't met her, she would probably still be floundering. She started to put feelers out to her various contacts at ACT UP and the ACLU about going to work for them—for pay—when the terrorist attacks of September 11 occurred.

As the country reeled and mourned and prepared, uncertain of what would happen next, a surprising thing happened for Rachel. Instead of following her lifelong dream of helping people through activism from the inside out, she found herself possessed by a thought that bubbled up out of nowhere:

She wanted to do radio again.

She knew she could help people if she was on the radio, disseminating information backed by knowledge and fact and tempered with concern and more than a little bit of humor, which might just include a fart joke or two.

"I really, really wanted to be back on the radio," she said. "I wanted to be helpful, making announcements about blood drives and doing news bulletins. I'll read the AP wire, I'll do the weather, I'll do snow days, I don't care. I just wanted to be back in there."

She was in luck. In the wake of the attacks, times were uncertain. People were scared and confused, and they turned to others to discuss the news and also the rumors that ran rampant at the time. As a result, many of the small-market local radio stations that still relied on live deejays and announcers shifted their programming to become live 24/7 call-in shows.

"Everybody at that point had stopped playing music and stopped doing stupid morning zoo stuff," she said. "Anybody who had a job in broadcasting right after 9/11 became an information source. First it was [where to] volunteer and donate blood, then it was the start of the Afghanistan war. There was a lot to explain, and I wanted to be helpful."

"And perhaps more importantly: I missed the opportunity to explain stuff," she admitted.

So she called the program director at WRSI, a local station out of Northampton, which happened to be her favorite radio station. She introduced herself as the newsgirl who used to work at WRNX until about a year earlier, then asked if she could pick up any weekend or fill-in shifts. She even offered to work for free; that's how much she needed to be back in radio.

They gave her a few shifts here and there, and she relished the opportunity to dive back in and felt as though she was contributing something and being useful to people in a way that was immediately effective.

In case there was any doubt, Rachel made it clear to station managers from the beginning that she wasn't going to muffle her identity as an out lesbian and a political radical.

But within a few months, she had done such a great job that the station executives offered her the chance to anchor the morning drive show, *Big Breakfast*. Rachel was thrilled to be back in radio and set about putting her own stamp on the show.

Whereas previous hosts had run the show along typical morning zoo lines, given the tenor of the times and her desire to explain the news in clear tones, while occasionally injecting a bit of warped humor into the mix to make it easier to go down, the station soon gave Rachel free rein to shape her show however she wanted. In addition to providing her spin on the latest development on the terrorism front, she played her favorite music and regularly hosted local experts to discuss news and upcoming events around the Pioneer Valley.

On snow days, she had less than a minute to announce a cancellation or delay for more than seventy-five schools throughout the region, and she found the easiest way to get through it was in the machine-gun patter of a country auctioneer. Occasionally she used a sound effects device to provide additional embellishment. "One of our preschools was the Make Way for Ducklings School, and I'd play this big quacking sound effect," she said.

She was still getting paid minimum wage, and she was solely responsible for handling the sound board, producing segments after the show was over for the morning, and announcing the artist and songs she played. It was a constant juggling act, especially when she had to give away tickets to local performances.

"When I had to give away concert tickets, I would put on a long song—usually something from Miles Davis—lock the door to the basement studio, run upstairs, and stand in the median on the main drag in Northampton, holding out concert tickets. I would tell people: 'During this Miles Davis song, I will be on Main Street holding concert tickets; drive by and pick them up.' People would stop at the median and get the concert tickets from me."

The long song was crucial: "By the time the song was over, I would've been able to get a coffee, pee, hand out the tickets, and go back and have something to say."

She particularly appreciated the fact that no one was looking at her while she did her job. When she was working in the prisons, she had to be refined and intelligent—and in the conservative South she started with two strikes against her, since most people realized just by her appearance that she was a lesbian. "One of the liberating things about radio is that nobody cares what you look like," she said. "You can stand up, sit down, gesticulate, move around wildly, use a prop, anything you want.

You're just trying to be entertaining and informative and engaging. I think radio is probably good food for the soul in that way, because you can't be too self-conscious."

As before, even though she loved being on the radio, she wanted to get back into activism, both locally and on a wider basis. Despite her radio career and growing following, she still considered herself to be an AIDS activist first and foremost. After her radio shift was over for the day, she would spend the afternoon hours working for ACT UP and ALRP from home. Instead of flying off to Alabama, she turned her attention to doing activism through mostly online venues, running listservs on prison reform and helping to support other AIDS organizations via computer. Not only did she have a regular job for which she bore pretty much all the responsibility, but she didn't want to leave Susan for extended periods of time.

Even though her AIDS-related work wasn't hands-on, it somehow felt more fulfilling to her. "I started to get more and more into the work," she said. "It seemed less of a lark and more like what I needed to be putting my brain into."

She also branched out into different forms of activism. Just as with her radio show, she was able to reach more people: Writing freelance articles about AIDS would also reach a wider audience. She started to write for *POZ*, a magazine for people who were HIV positive; the publication featured profiles of people who were living with HIV, articles about upcoming drug and treatment options, and opinion and editorial columns. For the July/August 2003 issue, Rachel wrote a story entitled

"Time Out: Feds to Prisoners: Get Out of Jail, Get Counseling and Care," in which she described the advances made in HIV prison care since her doctoral dissertation had been accepted almost two years earlier.

At this point, with more than a decade of activism under her belt—and obviously judging from the calming influence of her relationship with Susan—Rachel had become far more prosaic about what activism could and couldn't achieve and what she personally was willing to do to fight injustice.

"Activism is figuring out that there is something that you want to be changed in the world," she said. "Then you figure out the connection between yourself and that trigger."

More striking, she was starting to regard being on the radio as much more than something fun to tide her over until she got a real job in the nonprofit world. Not only did she have a knack for live radio—listeners appreciated her quick wit and thoughtfully intelligent responses, and how she never talked down to anyone—but she was also helping people every morning that she was on the air. Traffic reports and school closings were small potatoes, perhaps, but she felt genuinely heartened at seeing the joy on the faces of her neighbors when she handed out tickets to a show at Northampton's Academy of Music Theatre.

She started to ponder her next step up the ladder: talk radio, which was a curious choice, since at the time talk radio was aimed primarily at listeners who favored sports and conservative politics. But through the radio industry grapevine she'd gotten wind of a new talk radio network that would be aimed at a different kind of audience.

The buzz about Air America was that it would be something that had never existed before, a nationwide talk radio network aimed at people who skewed progressive and liberal. Programming would be formatted like that at any other syndicated radio network, with a rotating roster of hosts conducting live shows with news, guest segments, and monologues, with a portion of the show devoted to call-ins. Though her bosses at WRSI had never categorized what Rachel was doing as "progressive talk radio," that's what she had essentially been doing since she first went on the air, albeit with some deep album cuts occasionally thrown into the mix.

When Rachel first heard of the new network, she was excited at the prospect of broadcasting her views to a larger audience, though she did initially hesitate because she appreciated being able to collect herself between on-air segments by playing the long version of a song. "The idea that I'd be on talk radio and the only break I'd have would be commercials and then you have to come back and talk some more seemed very difficult to me," she said. "That seemed like a very big leap."

But she decided to go for it, because she knew it would fit her like a glove, even though she had her doubts about her hire-ability because of her lack of national and talk-show host experience. "They had no business hiring me," she said.

Besides, part of her thought that if she didn't go for it, she might never get another chance. "I've never really aimed at anything in my life long-term," she admitted. "There's always something that I want to do next, and something that I want to work hard on now and I seek out things that I want to work hard on. And while radio was fun, it was also difficult, and I realized if I worked hard I might get better at it."

Besides, she was getting tired of bouncing around—or back and forth—between activism and radio. Could she focus on one thing that would allow her to have a forum while also helping people? Clearly, a radio show with a national platform seemed to be the ticket. "If there was ever going to be a chance for me to do this as a real gig," she said, this was it. "So I pulled out all the stops."

She sent tapes of her *Big Breakfast* show to some of the Air America producers and followed up with phone calls, and when she didn't hear back, she sent more tapes and made phone calls. "I kind of banged on doors and wouldn't take no for an answer," she said.

"I even had an ex-girlfriend who pretended she was in Al Franken's class at Harvard bring him tapes of my hosted music show," she said.

Veteran TV producer Shelley Lewis had come on board to help launch Air America and was one of the producers Rachel had bombarded with tapes. Lewis hit play and settled in to listen, fully prepared to hit eject after a couple of minutes. But she was intrigued by Rachel's delivery and obvious intellect, along with another quality that she had rarely encountered. "She had this incredible brightness of being, this sort of joy," said Lewis.

She picked up the phone and called Rachel, and they spoke for a few minutes. Within a half hour Rachel was in her car heading for Manhattan.

The interview was almost over before it began. When a team of producers asked her who her favorite radio personalities were, Rachel responded with Glenn Beck. A couple of the interviewers exchanged looks, and one of them archly asked her if she knew that Air America was aimed at a *liberal* audience. She told them that, yes, she realized that, before adding that she knew where she stood as an advocate of liberal values despite the fact that he was at the top of her list when it came to a skilled radio broadcaster, at least back in the days before he had his own TV program.

The interview progressed and Lewis and the others were suitably impressed. They invited Rachel to come on board starting in March 2004, when the network would officially launch.

She was on her way. Rachel had spent just over two years as the host of *Big Breakfast* when she gave notice, not only to the station managers but also to the groups she volunteered with. "One day, I was an AIDS activist, and the next day, I wasn't," she said.

It had been part of her identity for so long that she felt bittersweet about leaving it behind. Publicly she was thrilled at the idea of her new job, but privately she doubted that it would last beyond a few months or indeed if her skills would be up to snuff for a national audience.

She assigned her online duties to other volunteers, fully

expecting that she'd pick the reins back up six months down the road. But in the meantime, she looked forward to being able to air her views to a wider and much larger audience.

"I just want to be able to help explain things clearly," she said. "I can look at what's going on, see the important thing in the universe of news that you might not know about, and tell you what it is and why you might want to know about it. It's something I feel compelled to do, a blend of opinion and journalism, but for me it really is just one thing, which is explaining. I think it's helpful to have context, perspective, or an angle on something in order to understand it better."

She and Susan rented a tiny 275-square-foot apartment at 25 Leroy Street in the West Village and figured out their new life: Rachel would spend Monday through Friday in Manhattan, and Susan would head down later in the week to stay for a couple of days before they drove back to Massachusetts together on Friday night so they could spend a quiet, relaxing weekend in the country. "We essentially treat [the apartment] like a hotel room," she said.

She was on her way.

CHAPTER 6

Air America

Even before March 31, 2004, when Air America flipped the switch to go live on the air for the first time, the fledgling network had already made a huge splash.

The bill for the launch party approached $70,000 and attracted celebrities including Yoko Ono and Tim Robbins, who added a bit of sparkle to news accounts and feature stories about the new network.

The week before the official launch, *The New York Times Magazine* devoted a cover story to the new network, focusing on former *Saturday Night Live* funnyman Al Franken's benchmark show from noon to three, where he'd be directly competing with then-ranked number one conservative talk-show host Rush Limbaugh. Democratic strategist Paul Begala, who'd previously served as an adviser to President Bill Clinton, cheered on the new station and characterized the new attitude that Democrats had in the political world: "This year, 'liberal' and 'wimp' have become decoupled," he said. "Liberals are ready to fight."

And Air America would be the first round in the arsenal to be fired.

In 2004, the country was in the thick of a contentious Democratic presidential primary season; Howard Dean, John Kerry, and John Edwards were the top contenders. After several years of Republican reign—the 2002 midterms bucked the usual trend of earning seats in the nonpresidential party, which gave the Republican majority even more of a stronghold in Congress— Democrats were ready to come out fighting, both in politics and in their personal lives. Talk-show hosts Rush Limbaugh and Bill O'Reilly commandeered the conservative market, and liberals were hungry for a media entity that catered exclusively to them.

Air America Radio produced and managed new radio shows as part of the media company Progress Media's two prongs of liberal attack; the other was Equal Time Media, a separate company that would be in charge of running, purchasing, and/or leasing the stations that would run Air America programs. The first slate of stations to sign on in New York, Chicago, Los Angeles, and San Francisco would air original live programming from six A.M. to eleven P.M., Monday through Friday, with reruns making up the rest of the schedule. Progress Media also would allow individual stations to buy the rights to air one or more of the shows in their markets.

It was an ambitious plan, some said too ambitious. But the founders, investors, staff, and on-air talent all believed in the gospel of Air America, and in 2004 their primary missions were to make George W. Bush a one-term president, end the war in Iraq—which had just passed its one-year anniversary—and make some money while they were at it.

And the stakes were much larger than at a small-market Massachusetts station. "We were going to change the American landscape," said Rachel. "It was a huge deal, and it seemed much bigger than me."

"We weren't just waging a battle, we're competing for ratings."

For the first time in her life, Rachel was part of a team that backed her 100 percent and believed in the same things she did, as compared with her activist days, when she had to dial back on her rhetoric and kowtow to people whose political views were the polar opposite of hers.

But some had their doubts. "Six months ago I wouldn't have given a liberal radio network a dime's chance for success," John Zogby, a pollster and political adviser, admitted. "What motivates talk radio is heavy emotion. Liberals are usually too busy fighting one another, but we are really polarized today, and there is high emotion on the liberal side."

On April 1, 2004, at six o'clock in the morning eastern standard time, the first show, *Morning Sedition*, hosted by comic Marc Maron, went on the air. "Nobody knew what was going to happen with Air America when it started," Rachel admitted. "We didn't know if it was going to take off and be this big deal."

At first, Rachel was hired in pretty much the same capacity as her first radio gig at WRNX: the rip-and-read newsgirl on *Unfiltered*, airing from nine to noon, focusing on news, politics, and a good dose of the arts and culture. She'd be working alongside Lizz Winstead, co-creator of *The Daily Show*, rapper Chuck D of Public Enemy, and Laura Flanders, a progressive activist who was involved with the media watchdog group FAIR and had her own radio talk show in San Francisco.

"I was supposed to be the sidekick newsgirl who came in at the top of the hour and did cut-ins, like I used to do on my morning zoo show, telling what's going on in the news," said Rachel. While the show was still in the planning stages, she pushed the producers to give her more to do, but they viewed her lack of major market experience as a hindrance, despite the fact that both Chuck D and Lizz had worked only on TV, not radio.

Despite her diminished role, Rachel dutifully attended all the staff meetings and helped to plan the show, from deciding how many guests to feature on each show to what kind of music to play leading up to the commercial breaks. It wasn't long before it became apparent that Flanders would instead host her own weekend show, *The Laura Flanders Show*, airing on Saturday and Sunday evenings.

There wasn't a Plan B, and with a couple of weeks to go before the network launch, there wasn't a lot of time to find another host. Lizz was pondering who could possibly step up to the plate and take the third chair when her eyes landed on Rachel. "Why don't you do it?" she asked.

Unfiltered's first show aired on March 31, 2004, and the three cohosts quickly settled into their on-air and behind-the-scenes roles from the beginning: Rachel handled the news, Lizz booked the guests, and Chuck D served as the "wild card," who loved to tell jokes in between opining at length about various topics of the day. "Comically enough, I'm the straight man of the three," Rachel said.

There was definite chemistry among the three as they chatted, interviewed guests, and took phone calls for three solid hours. Rachel's fine-tuned radio chops were on display from day one; she often showed up her cohosts with the depth of her knowledge and an entertaining way of conveying it, but the other two didn't seem to mind.

She also won the respect of her cohosts early on. "If I go off on some emotional, crazed tangent, she always brings it back to the facts," said Winstead. And cohost Chuck D. concurred, stating that Rachel's talent as a radio host went leagues beyond most of the others he's worked with, and a big plus was that she was using her talent as a broadcaster to "represent that voice that's not heard."

In the beginning, Rachel doubted that she'd have much in common with either Lizz or Chuck D, but that was soon disproved by their affectionate and respectful back-and-forth. She particularly enjoyed bantering on air with Chuck D. "It's such a funny combination, but we love each other," she said. They also teased each other about what kinds of women they preferred. "We talk about girls, and though he and I have different tastes, we can appreciate the other's type."

Others at the network took notice of Rachel's skills. "It was pretty clear to us from the very beginning that there was something special about her," said Matthew Traub, who helped get Air America off the ground.

Despite the light banter and laughs, all three hosts soon discovered that doing a three-hour radio show five days a week could be a tough, exhausting slog. "Going in the studio is like going into surgery," said Rachel. "Once those studio doors close and the red light goes on, there's no turning back."

But Rachel was well on her way; plus, she loved her new job. But from the beginning, Air America was on shaky ground, and chaos and confusion behind the scenes was the rule from day one, complicated by insufficient funding. After all, it requires a significant investment to get a nationally syndicated network off the ground, along with convincing local stations in new markets to switch their entire program schedule to an unproven formula.

A major venture capitalist had pulled out just before the network's debut, and in the first month both the CEO and executive vice president in charge of programming quit the network. To make matters worse, two of the five stations that had committed to carrying Air America's full slate of programming had stopped airing programs because of a contractual dispute with the network that prohibited the station from airing anything but Air America programming.

With so much internal and external turmoil going on, the situation was turning into a real catch-22: new stations didn't want to sign on, and advertisers didn't want to commit to buy-

ing airtime with just a handful of stations and listeners. The network was on life support just a month after its splashy debut,
and employees started to think about jumping ship; after a few
paychecks bounced, accounting told employees to wait twenty-
four hours before depositing the next one.

In addition to the financial pressures, part of the early floundering at the network was clearly due to the collective inexperience of its hosts. Critics in the first weeks loved the novelty of
being able to tune in to a wide variety of liberal and progressive
programs 24/7. But the stress of filling hours of airtime every
day—it wasn't as easy as it looked—soon started to take its toll
on on-air staff, which was not a surprise given that few had any
real experience in radio. From the beginning, executives at the
network were determined to get everything up and running
quickly—which meant throwing unseasoned radio talent and
staffers on the air—so they weren't terribly surprised at receiving early feedback that the quality of the programming was
rather spotty.

Others had their doubts when it came to the long-term viability of Air America. "The impression one gets . . . is that it's
really more of a political campaign with contributors than a
radio business with investors," said Michael Harrison, editor
of *Talkers*, a trade magazine that covers the talk radio business.
"And radio is not a political machine; radio is a medium."

Rachel began to worry that there was a real possibility that
her self-proclaimed six-month experiment in national radio
would come to an end a lot sooner. Indeed, some staffers flew

the coop and others were laid off, while others tenaciously held on, determined to make a difference in Bush-era America.

But after the housecleaning and an injection of new investment, things began to settle down and Air America—and Rachel—started to gain significant traction. When President George W. Bush was reelected in November 2004, the still struggling network could have gone in one of two directions: Regular listeners could have figured theirs was a lost cause and they should throw in the towel; or the defeat would fire up the liberal base, increasing listeners and market share across the country.

Fortunately for Rachel—and for Air America—the latter attitude took hold. The network quickly reorganized, gaining new board members and managers who loosened up on the company's original goals of aiming to buy and lease radio stations—which ate up the bulk of the initial capital—and instead allowed independent stations to pick and choose from a customized and limited list of programs, instead of its previous 24/7 all-or-nothing approach. The network also received some desperately needed capital from private investment firms and individuals who were outraged by the political climate.

A year later, the network was on firmer ground. Programming was broadcast in almost fifty markets across the country, and listeners could tune in online as well as on Sirius and XM satellite radio stations.

"[Air America] has definitely raised awareness in the industry that there is a market for different political views," said Harrison.

Although the network had stabilized to some extent, the same couldn't be said of *Unfiltered*. When Air America offered stations the opportunity to take the cafeteria approach and pick and choose which shows they wanted to air, only about half the stations opted to continue to run the show. And then Lizz Winstead left not only the show but the network itself in early March 2005, leaving Rachel and Chuck D to run the show by themselves.

Unfiltered could have hobbled along a little longer, but then an odd savior arrived in the form of Jerry Springer, a veteran TV host whose top-rated syndicated 1990s *The Jerry Springer Show* covered a wide array of controversial tabloid topics at the time, from murder to affairs and homosexuality. Many shows were often punctuated by a violent free-for-all scramble, with fists thrown and chairs flying as a raucous studio audience egged on the guests.

In late 2004, Springer decided to do a daily radio show in addition to his TV show. *Springer on the Radio* debuted in January 2005 on a station in Ohio, but after a few months he wanted to syndicate the show to broaden his audience, and Air America viewed the acquisition as a chance to boost their audience. "Jerry said to us, 'You guys have all the white wine and cheese crowd, I can bring you the beer and pretzel folks,'" said Jon Sinton, president of Air America.

Executives at Air America were so eager to bring him on board that they let him pick his own time slot, and the one he wanted was the morning show from nine to noon. *Springer on the Radio* debuted on April 1 and ran until December 2006—airing on as many as fifty-three stations during the run. In the fall of 2006, he competed on *Dancing with the Stars* and lasted seven weeks, after which he decided to cancel the radio show; *DWTS* had elevated his visibility, and so many new opportunities were popping up that his daily three-hour stint on air was preventing him from profiting from them.

Unfiltered was history, with March 31, 2005 being the show's last day; they'd been on the air for exactly one year. The cancellation of *Unfiltered* turned out to be a blessing in disguise, because Air America wasn't done with Rachel, not by a long shot. The network decided to give her her own one-hour show. The only free slot in the schedule was five A.M., and she grabbed it. *The Rachel Maddow Show* launched on April 14, 2005, running between five and six A.M., which meant that her workday began at midnight since the entire show was scripted: She wrote every single word she uttered on the air, except for commercials and breaks.

"I'm not an ad-libber," she said. "When you say something, you'd better have something to say or you're wasting a lot of people's time."

But she also had control over the content of her show for the first time. So in addition to choosing the stories for the show, she could shape the tone, and in Rachel's world that meant mixing serious topics with humor that sometimes bordered on crass.

"I'm really interested in war and prison and genocide— yippee!" she said. "But . . . the challenge is to knit together my interest in the most morbid things alive and my interest in fart jokes."

She designed the initial format of the show to be patterned after a feature on *Unfiltered* called "Burying the Lede," where she'd throw the spotlight on a story she thought had been receiving inadequate coverage in both regional and national media. "We realized that 'Burying the Lede' was kind of a big part of the mission of this overall show," she said.

It didn't look as though Rachel would be returning to her activist work anytime soon.

CHAPTER 7

Taking Off

Aᴠᴛᴇʀ ɪᴛs ʀᴏᴄᴋʏ first year, Air America had finally stabilized, increasing its reach from five to sixty-seven stations across the country, with an average of 3.3 million radio listeners, along with another 3.5 million tuning in via the XM and Sirius satellite networks as well as online.

Ratings had gotten a boost as George W. Bush won a second term in office. "What happened on November second may have been bad for America, but it sure was good for Air America," said Rob Glaser, a significant investor in Air America and chairman of the board.

In addition to having a Republican president for another four years, another reason for Air America's improved ratings was that the talent bookers at cable networks such as CNN and MSNBC were always eager to book guests and panelists who might break out into an on-air fistfight.

"When Air America was founded, all the bookers in cable

TV thought, We've got a new stable of liberals," said Rachel. "We already have the conservatives, and the people who work for Air America, you can count on the fact that they'll be liberal. Get a left-wing person and a right-wing person, and they can fight to the end of the show."

Of course, Air America expected that having their talk-show hosts appear on a national cable TV show would build their audience, so they strongly encouraged hosts to accept the bookings.

"I thought it was funny to be asked," said Rachel. "[I have] a face made for radio, if there ever was one."

But she accepted, and for her first appearance on CNN, Rachel was matched up with G. Gordon Liddy, a lawyer and FBI agent who was involved in the Watergate scandal during Richard Nixon's presidency and served fifty-two months in federal prison as a result. Right before they went on the air, Rachel said she couldn't help thinking, Hey! You were in prison when I was born.

She held her own on the show, and soon bookers at other shows on CNN and MSNBC started calling, including one who matched her up against Pat Buchanan, the right-wing pundit who gave the cultural war speech at the 1992 Republican convention that had served as a call to arms for Rachel more than a decade earlier.

Instead of rejecting the request outright, Rachel was curious about how he'd regard her on live TV. "When they picked me to fight with Pat Buchanan, I thought it was hilarious," she said.

She agreed, eager to debate her foil, and prepared for the worst. But he surprised her.

"He asked me hard questions, listened to my answers, took my answers seriously, and took time to rebut me," she said, adding that she respected his debating skills. He excelled at defending his opinions, despite the fact that she disagreed with them. "He listens to people who disagree with him and he's not condescending."

After their first matchup, the show cut to a commercial break. Buchanan thought Rachel had signed off from the network connection, and he started chatting with the host. But Rachel was still listening, and she overheard him say, "I like that liberal girl."

The networks obviously liked the pairing as well, because when Buchanan was booked for future on-air debates, they frequently acquiesced to his request for Rachel to represent the opposite side.

She, in turn, quickly viewed him not as a hardheaded far-right buffoon to conquer on air, but as a polite, older gentleman who went out of his way to help her, in part because he liked sparring with her. Rachel, for her part, enjoyed him because he was old-school, not sucking up to network brass to get ahead, but also not putting people down because they held opposite opinions.

"[Also] he's funny and quick and intellectually coherent, even when his views are totally toxic," she noted.

"And that's how he became Uncle Pat," which spawned a long on-air relationship that surprised bookers and hosts and built up her fan base, in part because their debates were not what most people expected. After all, not only was her content compelling and highly intelligent, but her delivery was well reasoned, even calm at times.

With "Uncle Pat," Rachel was proving that it would be a mistake for anyone to try to put her into a well-defined box, and she bristled whenever someone labeled her as a cookie-cutter liberal. "I don't feel like I am coming from a partisan wing of the American polity," she said. "I feel I'm a centrist; I try to have a respectful, traditionalist, moderate take on things. In the broader media world that makes me a raving liberal."

But not everyone appreciated the fact that she refused to toe the strict liberal party line. For example, Rachel didn't exactly endear herself to the political groups that most assumed would fall solidly into her camp: feminists and lesbians and gays. It was precisely because she refused to typecast herself—and continued to debate Pat Buchanan without accusing him of wanting to return women to the 1950s—that she encountered some resistance from liberal groups. "I'm not a consensus builder," she said. "I think that there is a wussy bias in feminist politics that doesn't make room for people like me."

At the same time, she did have her complaints about being on TV. "They see me as a novelty, because I've slipped through the cracks, this butch dyke," she said. "They always try to bring up gay marriage with me. We're talking about Syria, Bosnia, Rwanda refugees, on CNN and they're like 'Rachel, now how does this relate to gay marriage?'"

She also found fault with the abbreviated aspect of television. "It's frustrating sometimes that everything on TV is a sound bite," she said. "You can't explain Iran in fifteen seconds, but it does force you to get right to your point."

She used her radio experience to compare and contrast. "When you are doing radio, you're just talking right into some-body's ear, so you have to be a real person. On TV, you have to be looked at, so you have to be a thing."

And it was the things, or "elements" in TV parlance—that is, the *vision* part of *television*—that Rachel struggled with most after her years in radio. "I don't think visually at all, so I don't think about the visual elements," she admitted. "I think in terms of script, in terms of when stuff should pop up and when it shouldn't, and when things should be revealed on the show."

The overemphasis on how women were required to appear on camera was another visual aspect of TV that Rachel was never crazy about. "I know I don't look like everybody else on television," she said. "I'm not that pretty."

In her early appearances she tried to make this point by re-jecting any and all swipes of a makeup brush, but she quickly reversed course. "When I saw myself on TV, it was like Nixon debating Kennedy, so now I say, 'Do me up like you'd do a dude.' And they're like 'But you're so pretty, why would you want to look like a man? How about a little lip gloss?' And I'm like 'Hey, look. I look this way on purpose!'"

She also discovered that her following was growing expo-nentially, which also meant she learned to accept total strangers offering their unsolicited opinions on her sound bites as well as her physical appearance, explaining that a disproportionate number of TV viewers will feel free to comment, compared to radio listeners who tend to offer significantly less feedback, if any at all.

A few months after her first TV appearance, *The Situation with Tucker Carlson* debuted on MSNBC in June 2005 and Rachel became a regular guest commentator on the show. Carlson had previously cohosted CNN's *Crossfire*, featuring knockdown, drag-out fights between commentators on the left and the right, the exact kind of exchange that Rachel abhorred. After CNN announced its decision to cancel the show in January 2005, Carlson moved to MSNBC and took his show in a brand-new direction, partly because of Rachel. "She was completely fun to talk to, doesn't take political differences personally, but more than that, she's fast—really fast," said Carlson.

"She could spar intellectually with Tucker, but it never became unpleasant," said Bill Wolff, an executive producer on the show. "She doesn't seem to have any spite for people who disagree with her."

Many viewers—and critics—reacted enthusiastically. "What Maddow gives us in her few moments with Carlson is a kind of ultra-smart older sister whose jabbering smart-aleck brother isn't ever going to fool her—or lose her indulgent affection, either," wrote Jeff Simon of *The Buffalo News*.

"The reason to watch *The Situation with Tucker Carlson* is the program's decision to have Air America radio host Rachel

Maddow represent the left," wrote Ken Tucker of *New York* magazine. "Maddow, unlike *Crossfire*'s toothless hacks Paul Begala and James Carville, actually articulates leftist, progressive, sometimes even radical ideas. This immediately distinguishes her from everyone else on television since Abbie Hoffman circa *The Dick Cavett Show*."

Part of the reason she was so good on TV was that—sound bites aside—she viewed it as an extension of radio, because she actually didn't watch television.

In fact, she and Susan didn't own a TV, in either their Massachusetts home or their New York apartment. It wasn't because they looked down on programming, but because Rachel fully realized that it was dangerous for them to be in the same room with a television since if they turned it on they would succumb to whatever was on. "I am very easily distracted by flashing lights," she admitted. "If there is a TV on in the room, I won't eat, I won't sleep, I'll just meld with my couch."

Her unfamiliarity with popular political shows ironically turned out to be a major strength: "I don't know how you're *supposed* to be political on television," she said.

In addition to her work with Carlson, Rachel made the rounds at other shows and networks, and once the 2006 midterm elections began to heat up, she regularly appeared on Paula Zahn's show on CNN.

Though these appearances first and foremost served as

promotion boosters for her own show and for Air America as a whole, Rachel also viewed them as another step on the ladder that she had been moving up since her *Big Breakfast* days; she didn't deny that she hoped hosting her own TV show lay somewhere down the road.

She also wanted to have a bigger part in steering the course of the show. "The *Tucker* show made me pine for having a role in picking the topics," she said. "Story selection is half the battle, and more than half the fun."

Executives and producers at the various networks realized Rachel was destined for greater things, but they soon discovered that she didn't easily fit into any of the expected formats. CNN—which at the time leaned more to the right than to the left—brought her on board to make a pilot for a weekend show, but it didn't work; with Rachel's political views, it was like trying to squeeze a square peg into a round hole. "You wouldn't put *The Sopranos* on Comedy Central," said Jon Klein, CNN's president at the time.

And while many guests would cram for days for a segment that might last three or four minutes tops, scripting answers in advance to meet any possible angle an opponent might come up with, Rachel took a different approach. "I always think when it comes to a screaming match, there is always going to be someone who can scream louder than me, and frankly, I think I am unattractive when I scream," she said.

But she definitely appreciated the value of good theater on TV, especially with "Uncle Pat," because she knew their meet-ups would never deteriorate to an on-air fistfight. In addition, both were inveterate debaters who shared an honest love of the craft. "When Pat is saying something outrageous, you know when you yell at the TV? I get to yell at him in person," she said.

She realized that she had to excel on these shows, because she was, more often than not, simply outnumbered. This effectively moved the needle well past the center when it came to political opinion since more often than not, the talent bookers on the shows would obviously pick guests who skewed to the right, telling Rachel they invited her onto the shows . . . "for balance."

As was the case with her relationship with Buchanan, despite their opposite views Rachel wasn't shy about voicing her respect for Carlson. "Tucker has been incredibly personally kind to me, and professionally generous to me," she said. "He put me on that show knowing from the beginning that we were going to fight every single day, and that I was going to give him a really good run for his money and sometimes beat him. I think Tucker deserves a lot of credit for that."

She was also learning that a good part of the dog-and-pony show in which she was participating was just good old-fashioned show business. "Off camera and off microphone, I've found that some of these types will often admit they don't really believe the stuff they say in public," she said.

As was the case in her early radio days, there was still a vocal group of people who disparaged Rachel for being a lesbian.

During the 2006 congressional race in Ohio, Democratic candidate Zack Space went on Rachel's radio show to talk about his positions. Afterward, his Republican opponent, Bob Ney, sent an email and made a robocall to voters painting Space as ultra-liberal simply because he appeared on the show. Ney then referred to Rachel as a "cross-dressing lesbian" and a "transgender king."

Rachel initially found the incident amusing and poked fun at it. "Perhaps he does not like ladies to wear pants?" she pondered. "My girlfriend is a femme and doesn't wear pants, and I know that's controversial in some areas, but I don't know what a cross-dressing lesbian or a transgender king is. I'm sure I'm for either, though."

But she knew full well there was always the danger that someone who was homophobic might take things a bit too far and attack her with more than words. She acknowledged that she had received letters and calls threatening violence and even death against her. After initially joking about the email and robocall, she started to worry. "One of these call recipients, some kook, might decide to do something about me," she admitted. "That was unsettling."

In addition, despite her great success and growing following, Rachel was still prone to an occasional bout of depression, and she admitted that it hindered her concentration. "It doesn't take away from my joy in my work or my energy, but coping with depression is something that is part of the everyday way that I live and have lived as long as I can remember," she said, adding that the emotional rush she experienced while doing her show didn't cut short the length of a depressive episode.

"I've been a pretty moody person ever since I was a kid, but I can't get that low when I'm on the air because of the excitement that I'm on the air," she explained. "I can be in the worst mood in the entire world, or tired, jet-lagged, or whatever, but when the theme music of the show comes on, I'm like, oh, hey, this is exciting."

When the "ON AIR" light goes off at the end of her radio show, the depression quickly seeps back into her consciousness. "When I'm depressed, it's like the rest of the world is the mother ship and I'm out there on a little pod and my line gets cut, and I don't connect with anything, I just sort of disappear."

Over the years, she's tried the usual ways to deal with it, from distraction to regular therapy sessions, but it took her a while to discover that her depression had a chemical basis, and she learned to anticipate its arrival when she couldn't detect certain smells. "It has nothing to do with anything else in your life," she said. "It's like a train and I just ride until it slows down enough so I can get off."

Eight months after getting her own solo show at Air America, Rachel graduated to a two-hour show starting at the more palatable hour of seven A.M. Never one to cut corners, after a year flying solo on the air, she had obviously hit her stride and reveled in each moment she had on the air, but in the back of her mind she realized it could be only temporary. "I keep expecting it to all fall apart, and go back to my life as an activist," she said.

Even with the expanded airtime, she still refrained from using her position as a bully pulpit of any kind. "I'm not [about] getting people to 'call your congressman to get this thing passed!' You can't say at the end of your broadcast day or at the end of your season, 'Did you win?'"

While other radio hosts would have taken advantage of the later start time to sleep in an extra hour or two, Rachel in fact doubled down on her workload because it meant she had twice as much airtime to fill. "It takes an incredible amount of time to prep every show," she said. "The rule of thumb in talk radio is that you prep for one hour for every hour on the air, but we do five hours for two hours, which is obscene."

She still wrote practically every word she uttered on the show—and typically covered twenty-three stories in seventy-four minutes—a fact she took great pride in. "I just don't have a rant and then open the phones," she said. "[It's a] super-fast-moving, content-rich, scripted, really highly produced show."

Her breakneck schedule was, however, taking a toll. When asked what she thought of her work schedule, she bluntly replied, "It blows. Even if you think of yourself as a night person, around four A.M. you want to go to bed, but that's when I'm having my news meeting and things are kicking into gear. It's a very strange, alienating lifestyle."

After she left the studio, she would head to a local restaurant, slide into a booth, and order a Bloody Mary, justifying it by saying, "It's your day, but it's my night."

Many relationships, conducted part-time and long distance, wouldn't have been able to withstand the hours, not to mention the fact that Rachel's profile continued to rise. But her relationship with Susan actually grew stronger as they established a weekly routine going back and forth between Massachusetts and New York, with Rachel heading down to New York via train on Sunday afternoons, Susan driving down on Wednesday, and the two of them returning on Friday night after the last show of the week.

Back in Massachusetts, Rachel felt she could relax and recover from her "always on" lifestyle in the city. She caught up on sleep, spent time with Susan and friends, went fishing in warmer weather, and basically relished the opportunity to enjoy the quiet and spread out; their living room in Massachusetts is twice as big as their 275-square-foot Manhattan apartment. "We can psychologically afford to live in a broom closet because we have this beautiful house to come back to," she said.

They also liked to have a little fun when they were out and somebody recognized Rachel's voice. Once she and Susan were eating at a diner, chatting away, and a couple of men were sitting in an adjacent booth. Suddenly the men's conversation stopped and one approached their booth and started talking to Susan. "I recognize you by your voice," he told her, at which point Rachel broke in and said, "That would be me. Thanks for listening!"

He quickly excused himself and returned to his booth. "He associated pretty voice, pretty girl, and here was this butch dyke!"

In fact, Susan was often approached by men when they were out together, which Rachel took in stride. In contrast, Rachel often was approached by gay men who thought she was a teenage boy. However she's also said that she's starting to get . . . what we call in the business "news ass." "I'm spreading out a little bit, which is hurting my I-look-like-a-seventeen-year-old-boy experience!"

News ass or not, she was on her way, and she wanted more.

CHAPTER 8

Punditry

Even though Rachel was still building her reputation and eager to give talks at association lunches and be interviewed at obscure lesbian publications with small readerships, she would automatically refuse a booking if the intent of her appearance was in any way salacious or if the only intent was for her to serve as the token lesbian.

On August 28, 2003, Madonna and Britney Spears had kissed onstage at the MTV Video Music Awards, which at the time was an unprecedented move at a live awards show or anywhere on national TV, for that matter. The buzz on talk shows and news programs was palpable, and Fox News invited Rachel onto one of their shows for her take on the matter.

When she got the call, "I thought that it was one of my friends calling me playing a joke," she said. For one, she viewed the request as fairly ridiculous: "What on earth do I have to say about that? I could go on and say, 'No comment, I don't have a take on that.'" But more so, she was somewhat insulted that it was the first time they wanted to book her and the topic was so superficial. "It was incredible to me that they were looking down their list of people they could potentially call and they decided, 'We've never called this woman before, but on this story, she'll be perfect!'"

At the same time, she never passed up a chance to be subversive and catch people off guard—not only viewers and listeners, but also the hosts and correspondents interviewing her—because they assumed she'd respond in a predictable manner. Instead, she always relished the chance to blow apart people's assumptions.

"My favorite thing is to watch panic ensue," she said, recalling a producer who booked her for her take on beauty pageants, thinking she'd come out against the tradition. "But I think beauty pageants are hilarious, I have no problem with them at all. I could come up with a feminist argument against them, but it's not what I'm focused on. So they booked me under the assumption that I would be railing against the ethics of beauty pageants and they put me on against somebody who was a participant's mom at a beauty pageant. When I didn't say what I was supposed to say, it was like there had been an electrical short in the studio: 'Go to commercial, go to commercial.' It was spectacular."

Rachel was an avid fan of *The Daily Show with Jon Stewart*, which changed everything about TV . . . and radio, as it turned out.

A 2004 poll conducted by the Pew Research Center for the People & the Press discovered that 21 percent of people between eighteen and twenty-nine turned to *The Daily Show*—along with *Saturday Night Live*—as their primary source for national news and to hear the latest on the presidential campaign.

Rachel occasionally watched the show online, carefully studying both how stories were chosen and how they unfolded over the course of its twenty-two minutes four nights a week. And she took careful notes about how to apply what she saw to her own show, explaining that by mixing the day's headlines with humor, Jon Stewart and his staff paved the way for her own show.

"You get more engaged with things if you're laughing and entertained," she said.

In fact, she was an early subscriber to this theory from her days on *Big Breakfast*. "I think that humor, sarcasm, and satire are one of the ways that you make people remember story lines and story arcs," she said. "Our brains are wired in a way so we tend to remember and absorb punch lines better than we remember thesis statements. So I try to do both."

She cemented her respect for what Jon Stewart had accomplished by hiring former *Daily Show* writer Kent Jones for her radio show. Jones had started working on other shows at Air America around the same time as Rachel and even wrote some of the content for *Unfiltered*. He had written for *The Marc Maron Show*—which had replaced *Morning Sedition*—until the summer of 2006, when he joined Rachel as writer and occasional cohost.

Her schedule eased up somewhat when Tucker Carlson's time slot shifted and he used the opportunity to move the show to Washington, D.C. Rachel appreciated the extra time but also respected the opportunity the show had provided and how he had treated her. "He's a very considerate person who was nice to work with and really good to his staff," she said. "It was a really good experience for me and I'm happy to have had it."

Rachel looked for more opportunities to fill the gap, among them the elusive holy grail of having her own TV show, but only if she could have complete control over the content. "I would love to be doing something in a medium where I get to control what I talk about." She admitted that the odds were long: "That's really hard to get, especially when you're an out, commie dyke."

She had already become aware of the standard dynamic at other cable channels and how they reflect the political views of higher-ups, particularly with Rupert Murdoch and Fox News. "Sometimes executives—occasionally hosts—will decide that they desire a political outcome in the world, so they create a story that they think will achieve a political outcome and then just drive it and drive it and drive it, as a political operation," she said.

In late 2006, Rachel also had to concern herself with the fact that she might have even more free time in the near future, because Air America—which had never been able to achieve financial self-sufficiency since its early troubled days—filed for bankruptcy in October, pledging to reorganize and secure sufficient finances for the future. Even though it had gained a total of ninety-two affiliate stations across the country, cranking out nineteen hours of original shows every day was a very expensive proposition, especially in a year without a presidential election to fire up the base. Listener numbers and market share continued to plummet.

"Liberals were not wired to listen to AM talk radio," Rachel acknowledged. "AM radio is religion, sports, and people yelling about immigrants, so liberals don't even know that AM is part of the radio. We're trying to meet a need that does not exist."

Still, she continued to put her all into every show while also keeping an eye out for other possibilities; she started to focus on the upcoming presidential campaign season that began in early 2007 as possible candidates began to test the waters in Iowa, New Hampshire, and other early primary and caucus states.

And then Keith Olbermann came calling. On his *Countdown* show on MSNBC, he had developed a reputation for skewering far-right political figures in the Bush administration as well as Fox News host Bill O'Reilly. While his approach was definitely different from O'Reilly's—he never hesitated to hide his animosity—he thought Rachel could provide another viewpoint for his program. She started to make guest appearances on the show, and he was so impressed that he suggested to his producers that she serve as guest host whenever he was away on assignment or taking a short vacation.

They readily agreed. Like Olbermann, they were impressed by her energy, wit, and snappy comebacks. But she wanted a firmer commitment; throughout 2007 she was still making appearances on both CNN and MSNBC, and executives at both networks were not happy about her hopping around. She called MSNBC's bluff, telling them, "If you're not going to marry me, I'm not going to stop dating."

In early 2008, MSNBC offered Rachel an exclusive contract to appear on the network, so she said goodbye to CNN and committed to MSNBC in the hopes that she would prove her mettle enough for the network to one day give her a show of her own.

Bill Wolff of MSNBC, for one, wasn't surprised. "Rachel is the universal donor of good chemistry," he said. "You can put her on to talk to just about anybody about just about anything, and she comes across as just so cheerful and hopeful and likable."

One problem: She had never used a teleprompter before, so Olbermann taught her.

"She mastered it in ten minutes but then started asking questions I didn't have answers for, like 'How do you keep from looking like you're reading?' And 'What's your purpose in looking away and reading quotes from the script?'

"I don't think she made one mistake in her first hour using one live on national television," Olbermann said, while admitting that he made several each night even after he had been on the air for several years.

"In the pundit world I'm the liberal [that] conservatives like, which is very unsettling," Rachel said, adding that this likability is a real by-product of coming out as a lesbian when she was a teen: She believes that developing a sense of diplomacy as a result has helped her smooth out her dealings with people with beliefs on the other side of the fence. "It's a talent that gay people bring to everything we do," she said.

"I believe one hundred percent that the reason I have not gone further in television is not only because I am gay, but because of what I look like," she said at the time.

She continued her friendly on- and off-air relationship with Pat Buchanan, sparring with him on a regular basis in 2008 as the presidential primary season heated up. They sat next to each other in the MSNBC show *Race for the White House*, a new program that started in March and aired Monday through Friday at six P.M., anchored by David Gregory, the chief White House correspondent for NBC News.

For Rachel, the show broadened her audience, and she allowed herself to dream what it would be like to have her own show. But she wasn't holding her breath.

She admitted that the Democratic primary—by June it was a contest between Barack Obama and Hillary Clinton—was a big part of the reason the networks were clamoring for her to appear on a wide variety of shows. "With this long, interesting, raving extravaganza of a Democratic primary with a white woman and a black man as the two major contenders, I think that it created a sort of affirmative action impulse for pundits," she said.

Of course, whether she appeared on a conservative or liberal show, it didn't take long for the host and/or other panelists to press her to reveal whom she preferred; most assumed that she supported a straight Democratic ticket. But again refusing to be pigeonholed—and confounding people on both left and right—Rachel declined to make her choice public. "I have never [thought] and still don't think of myself as an Obama supporter, either professionally or actually," she said. "[I feel] liberated by having a professional role in which it's probably better for me not to take sides."

In addition to her appearances on *Countdown* and *Race for the White House*, she offered commentary for special coverage on other MSNBC shows such as *Verdict with Dan Abrams* on primary nights throughout the winter and spring.

Rachel was also racking up accolades from a variety of media: *The Nation* magazine included her on its Most Valuable Progressives list, while the British newspaper *The Telegraph* named her one of the fifty most influential political pundits in America.

As the conventions approached in the summer of 2008, she visited the *Today* show, and both *New York* magazine and *The New York Times* raved about her in gushy profiles; she was quick to point out their errors, as when *The New York Times* used the word "sunny" to describe her personality. "Sunny and buoyant, I wouldn't describe myself as being," she said. "And nobody wants to be buoyant; it is just a shade shy of dim."

But the media attention definitely suited her subversive

streak. "I love the idea that I am the voice of woman," she said. "Look at me, I look like a dude."

And her humor and folksy demeanor endeared her to reporters and interviewers. But she never stopped being hard on herself. If anything, as her visibility increased, so did her self-criticism. For one, she thought that she would have at least one book under her belt by this time, maybe two, and that she'd have her own blog in addition to contributing to others while also pursuing her dream of having her own TV show. Instead, she had long ago discovered that radio was a full-time endeavor, requiring everything she could throw at it, and more.

"Rachel has always worked really, really hard," said Susan.

"I have been a suicidal, stretched-too-thin, overcommitted, frenetic, sleepless mess for the entire time she has known me," Rachel admitted. "I think the reason that I worked hard is that it makes me feel like my life has meaning."

Despite her success, old habits die hard. "I'm motivated in every half second of every minute of every hour of every day by fear of failure, which causes me to do extra reading and preparation."

Air America emerged from bankruptcy, and the new owner bought the network for a measly $4.25 million in 2007. While it was still not anywhere close to being financially solvent—after Al Franken's paycheck for $360,749 bounced, the new owner refused to cover the check—the network wanted to make sure that people knew who had given Rachel her first big break and that they were sticking by her; they were obviously nervous about losing their star. "We've seen the potential for greatness in Rachel for years," said Air America chairman Charles Kireker. "We view her as a homegrown talent, and hope and expect to have her continue hosting a radio show on Air America for a long time."

But Rachel was obviously setting her sights higher: She made no secret of the fact that she wanted a TV show of her own.

"[MSNBC] knows I would love to do it," she said. "I'm going to let them decide what they want to do about me."

"At some point, I don't know when, she should have a show," Phil Griffin, the president of MSNBC, said in July 2008. "She's on the short list. It's a very short list and she's at the top."

For her part, Rachel didn't totally rule out the idea of hosting a TV show and continuing to keep one foot in radio. "If O'Reilly, Hannity, and Beck can [host both], so can I," she said.

But for the time being, she kept up her breakneck schedule of juggling radio and TV appearances. "I'm saying yes every time they ask me to be on television," she said.

And then Keith Olbermann went on vacation.

Rachel, of course, was his first choice—as well as the network's—to fill in for him for eight nights in all, starting on July 2, 2008.

She had grown comfortable subbing for Olbermann on *Countdown* on occasional nights here and there and had developed her own style, with a little more wit and mild sarcasm than Keith. "Trying to do it as if I'm Keith isn't the best way to go," she said.

Rachel enjoyed the run, but when it ended on July 14, she was resigned to returning to her scattershot schedule while she waited for a show of her own to materialize.

CHAPTER 9

A Show of Her Own

WHEN GUEST HOSTS fill in for a vacationing host, ratings typically drop well below what they are when the star is in residence. But after Rachel finished her guesting stint on *Countdown* and the numbers came out, everyone took notice, especially the executives at MSNBC, when the audience numbers during her stint maintained Olbermann's figures.

"After we saw that, it was pretty clear that Rachel would get an audience after Keith," said Phil Griffin.

She would get her wish a lot sooner than later. In fact, just one month after she wrapped up, MSNBC in the *New York Times* on August 19, 2008, announced that Rachel would get her own show at 9 P.M., the hour following *Countdown*.

Though Griffin had made the official announcement, it was primarily Olbermann who brought her on board. Jeff Zucker, the CEO of NBC Universal—the parent company of MSNBC—wanted to keep his star happy, referring to *Countdown* as "one of the signature brands of the entire company." After all, Olbermann had recently re-upped at the network with a four-year contract worth $4 million a year, and MSNBC was determined to keep him happy.

Countdown was rebroadcast at 10 P.M. Olbermann wanted a strong show that would provide an audience who would not change the channel before ten o'clock, when his show was replayed.

Rachel was ecstatic, thrilled that her dream would finally come true.

Her new show would debut on September 8, 2008—exactly a month after the 2008 Summer Olympics launched—to coincide with the post–Labor Day media scrum leading up to Election Day and the election of a new president, "the final leg of the political race this year," said Griffin.

After a brief celebration with Susan, Rachel got to work; her workload had essentially just doubled. Not only did she have to lay the groundwork for a new show, but she was planning to continue her program on Air America. In addition, MSNBC decided to showcase its new find by providing Rachel with plenty of opportunities to appear at the upcoming Democratic National Convention, running from August 25 through 28 in Denver.

She appeared throughout the convention coverage, offering on-camera political analysis and commentary, presiding over various forums, and interviewing delegates, but she was eager to knuckle down on what she described as a "four-night infomercial."

The pumpkin Rachel helped carve for the annual high school Halloween celebration won first place for the freshman class.

Castro Valley High School Yearbook, 1987

Rachel's skills — not to mention her height of six feet — helped contribute to her team during her sophomore year.

Castro Valley High School Yearbook, 1988

As secretary of the Associated Student Body in her senior year, Rachel strikes a casual pose for a 1990 yearbook photo.
Castro Valley High School Yearbook, 1990

Rachel all glammed up for her senior year yearbook photo.
Castro Valley High School Yearbook, 1990

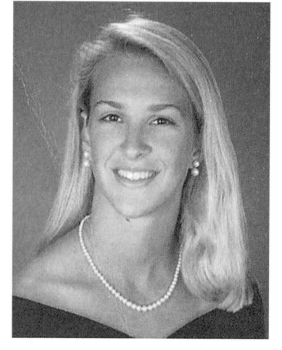

Rachel photographed in San Francisco in December 1994. Weeks earlier she had received the news that she was named a Rhodes Scholar for the following year. *Copyright Rick Gerharter*

Rachel Maddow at a 2005 appearance to promote Air America in New York City.
Angela Jimenez

In October 2005 Rachel was developing a following as a result of her Air America gig, and fans were flocking to her public appearances.

Creative Commons

The Rachel Maddow Show broadcast from Afghanistan in July 2010. Here she speaks with Lt. Col. Andy Gerlach, Brigade Executive Officer with the 196th Maneuver Enhancement of the South Dakota Army National Guard.

Photo by Sgt. Rebecca Linder of the 196th Maneuver Enhancement Brigade / DVIDSHUB.net

Rachel prepares cocktails during her appearance on *Diggnation* at the MSNBC.com Digital Café in June 2009.

Eric Susch / Flickr / Creative Commons

Rachel working with her beloved whiteboard during a staff meeting in 2010.

Christopher Anderson / Magnum Photos

Rachel with her parents, Elaine and Robert, and her brother, David, at a reception for Susan Mikula's gallery opening in February 2010.

Rachel and Susan at a reception for Susan's gallery opening in February 2010.

Rachel arriving at the Ed Sullivan Theater for an appearance on the *Late Show with David Letterman* in August 2011.

Henry Mcgee-Globe Photos, Inc.

Rachel and Susan at a reception for Susan's opening in March 2011.

Brian Cahn / Zumapress.com

Rachel and Susan celebrate after purchasing artwork from Ward Schumaker in February 2010.

She'd be taking over the time slot of *Verdict with Dan Abrams*, whose host took a more temperate tack than Olbermann and focused on exploring the legal issues of any particular topic. The departing host took the news diplomatically, at least out in public. "Considering where the network is right now, it is actually the right call," he said.

After the convention ended, Rachel dove right in, but the transition got off to a rocky start. First of all, in the interests of the tight schedule, the *Verdict* staff would transfer over to her show. Second of all, Rachel had very high standards for what she expected from the staff; her aim was first and foremost to create a show that would serve as an accurate representation of who she was as a person while steering clear of the lowest-common denominator methods popularly employed by other news-oriented shows of the time.

"[They're] like being put through a meat grinder and coming out as a pasteurized and homogenized meat product," she said. "I want to remain a veal chop."

Wolff invited the staff to a party the night before her debut, and a couple of hours in, Rachel tapped on her wineglass to give a speech to rally the troops.

She welcomed them all and said she looked forward to working with everyone, but things quickly went downhill when she proceeded to explain the format and approach that her new show would take—essentially that it would be the polar opposite of *Verdict*. When she said, a bit jovially, "Forget everything you've learned," faces fell throughout the room.

"Everyone was pale," said Susan. "It could not have been more of a bummer. Or more quiet."

Though Rachel had intended her statement to emphasize to her new staff that they needed to shift their approach from the whiplash-inducing frenzy of the ever-changing news cycle to a more thoughtful one, she knew she had screwed up.

She justified it by saying all she wanted to do was to win people over to her side. "I'm trying to say, 'Here's how I see the world,'" she said and "I think that we can make sense of this world together."

Suitably chastened, she headed in to work the next day, the first day of her new job, and got to work.

Despite the discomfort her staff felt toward her—and vice versa—*The Rachel Maddow Show* was a hit from day one, debuting on September 8, 2008, with 1,543,000 viewers, almost double what her predecessor, *Verdict*, had been generating. And just a week later, on September 16, 2008, the show drew 1,801,000 viewers—with 534,000 in the highly desirable 25–54 demographic—becoming the most-watched show on MSNBC at night.

Within two months, ratings were averaging an audience of 1.9 million a night, a feat that usually took at least a couple of years to achieve, if at all. After that, the sky was the limit, especially since Rachel was outranking talk-show veteran Larry King's program on CNN, which hadn't occurred in more than twelve years.

When it came to explaining her show's runaway success, Rachel was more modest, offering kudos to other influences, particularly the homestretch of an extremely contentious presidential campaign.

"I opened an umbrella factory at the start of monsoon season," she said. "Everybody's ratings went up, and for me to have stepped in at that moment, immediately after the conventions, made me look like a genius. I was getting explosive ratings, but so was everybody else. I think I benefited from being the new kid in that environment, and Keith Olbermann's ratings are off the charts so I have the best lead-in in cable news."

It could also have been due partly to the fact that she was the first out lesbian to host a prime-time cable news show, a factor that she brushed aside. "I can't be less gay, but being the first *blank* is always important," she said.

But she scoffed whenever a fan or critic referred to her as an overnight success. "I have always aspired to the Lucinda Williams model of overnight sensation," she said, "which is the fifteen-year hard slog overnight sensation, which is that you've been doing the work for a very, *very* long time, and then ultimately somebody notices you who doesn't realize you've been doing that work for that long. And they call you an overnight sensation and claim your success."

Unlike her predecessor—and other hosts at MSNBC and elsewhere—Rachel took great pains not to underestimate her audience. "There's been an idea in American media, that people don't really want anything that's going to make them think, and I just don't think that's true," she said. "I think Americans are smart, and you can sort of do graduate school–level work as long as you're willing to explain things and assume people can come along with you."

At the same time, while she had never tried to hide her intelligence, she knew full well that a preponderance of other cable TV hosts tended to play down their smarts on air; she wouldn't be among them. "I realized I didn't have to be afraid to be smart, and the audience can be there with me. I think there's room for all sorts of different kinds of discourse, including satire, including teasing, including humor. There's a lot of different ways to talk about stuff, and Americans absorb information in a lot of different ways," she said.

"With information becoming cheap, the success of Rachel and Keith is because people want someone collating or commenting on information," said Wolff.

As a condition of employment, Rachel told MSNBC that she had to have total control over the tone and content of the program, or else it wouldn't work. Indeed, in all the years she's hosted the show MSNBC has never objected to any of her content, keeping their approach hands-off.

"My whole thing is to let Rachel be Rachel," said Wolff.

She was amused by the public perception that occasionally assumes otherwise. "I get a lot of feedback from people who say they support me, but they're sorry that I'm constrained by my corporate tethers and I'm not allowed to talk about whatever this person wants me to be talking about, but that's all on me," she said. "If I'm not talking about something that you want to be talked about, it's my fault, not the corporate network's fault."

The critics—at least the left-leaning media—raved. "Maddow's deep, modulated voice is reassuringly calm after so much shrill emotionalism and catfights among the channel's aging, white male divas," said Alessandra Stanley in *The New York Times*.

Over at *Slate*, reviewer Troy Patterson said this: "She's confident enough in the intelligence of her arguments not to attempt bludgeoning anyone with them."

"Rachel blew up as huge as I've ever seen someone in the media sphere," said Matthew Polly, a fellow Rhodes Scholar whose years at Oxford coincided with Rachel's. "Suddenly there were profiles of her in every major magazine and she was on all the talk shows. It was like a comet, I've never seen anything like it, going from relatively unknown to major politico pundit in such a short order."

In addition to high ratings, accolades and awards began to pour in from various media outlets. *Politico* named her to their annual Top 10 Political Newcomers list and *The Washington Post* pegged her as a Breakout Star of 2008. And *Out* magazine named her the fourth most powerful gay person in the United States; Barney Frank, Ellen DeGeneres, and Anderson Cooper took the spots in front of her.

But there was trouble in paradise. Despite the praise and doubled viewership, some employees were still feeling bitter toward Rachel, not only because of her speech the night before her debut, but because they had to change practically everything about the way they did their jobs.

There were also signs that she was having trouble adjusting to being the head of a larger news organization than she was used to; after all, when she was working in radio she worked with just three other staffers, tops. "I don't know how to work with a big staff of people," she admitted. "It's the difference between writing your own blog and running a publication where you've got multiple writers, you've got information coming in from other sources, and you've committed to things in advance that you've got to get done on time. That element of it is really hard."

And juggling everything in her schedule—including appearances and interviews with other media to promote the new show—was proving to be a challenge. "I still haven't really figured out when I'm supposed to be where, and how to make sure there's time in every day to do things like eat and sleep and read my email," she said.

She was also still doing her radio show every day, which meant she was stretched extremely thin. And as was the case with her radio show, she insisted on scripting almost every word of her TV program, at least the segments where it was just her speaking to the camera, no guests, no graphics, no news clips.

"In broadcast journalism, the camera's a little bit like an X-ray, and you can tell if the person on camera has come up with their own ideas, or if they're just reading something that somebody else wrote for them," she said.

"But I'm a bad actor, so I can't do that. I do my own research and my own writing. I get fact-checked and I receive drafts from producers, but I really am doing all my own work every day. Better broadcasters than I am can fake it, and make you believe that they did the work themselves when they don't actually know what they're talking about. But when I don't know what I'm talking about, it shows."

In the same vein, Rachel was determined to shape her new program by consciously veering away from topics that other media were already covering, as well as the way they were covering it. "I don't just think about what people are already interested in, because it's probably something that other people are trying to explain or answer for them already," she said, adding that before she decides to cover any story on the show, she asks one simple question: How can we add more useful information to a particular story?

"Unless we are adding something that people don't already know, it's likely we will bore our audience," she said. "It's [also] a strategy for life, but I definitely think it's a strategy for news. There are stories that come up that people are really into where I can't add anything. So, we don't do it, even if it is a really important story."

From the show's early days, this "useful information" also

included some of Rachel's more "out there" ideas. Viewers couldn't get enough, tuning in every night to watch her factual yet opinionated presentations, along with the occasional wacky conspiracy theory that carried just enough merit to be a real possibility but was delivered in such a way that viewers weren't sure if she was messing with them, winking, or serious.

At the same time, some viewers were unhappy specifically because she was covering such a broad range of interests, as well as with the fact that even though she considered herself to be liberal, she was nonpartisan in her selection of stories. In other words, she didn't toe the party line on the program, and many were taken aback when she didn't view the show as an extension of her activist past.

"A lot of people tell me that what I'm doing on TV now is activism, but it's really not," she said. "What I'm doing right now is explaining stuff. Activism is finding something that is a way you want it not to be, figuring out who got to decide that it is that way, why it is they decided it should be that way, and [figuring out] what would change their mind. And then you set about making all of those things fall into place so that thing changes."

She maintains that the line between broadcasting and activism is a thick one, and while she's open to considering covering topics from her activist past, from prisons to AIDS to what's going on in Massachusetts, she stresses that the buck stops with her. "When someone . . . presents me with talking points, that guarantees that I will never use them."

In a way, even though she regularly pointed out that she was not a journalist, she respected journalists and regarded their standard procedures as a benchmark in developing principles for her own show, striving to be as transparent as possible. For one, when it came to having guests on the show, she clearly preferred journalists. "I have a bias toward reporters and experts rather than analysts," she said.

"We cite the source of the reporting and say where [a piece of] news came from," she added. "We also abide by NBC News rules and standards in terms of what we put on the air when we are working from other people's reporting that has not been independently corroborated by NBC News."

The Punch-and-Judy shows she participated in when she represented the liberal point of view were verboten when it came to her own show; she refused to spark on-air fights just for the sake of ratings, so for that reason, she rarely had two guests on in the same segment. If she couldn't examine an issue with another person as if it was a formal debate, she tended to pass.

And she set another precedent on cable news: Whenever she or a staffer made an error in a story, they ran a correction as soon afterward as possible. "We have a tradition in this country of newspapers running corrections, which should be done in every form of journalism," she said, admitting that somehow it comes out differently on television. "It is weird in television journalism to have somebody go on the air and say, 'I got this wrong,' or, 'I don't think I got this wrong, but people who are the subject of this report that I just did are complaining that it's wrong. Here's where they might have a point. Here's where they're not right.'"

Because she made a point of running corrections on a regular basis, she fully acknowledged that it provided critics of the show and network with ample ammunition. "With people who criticize MSNBC for ideological reasons, anytime anybody does a correction, they'll be like 'MSNBC did a correction, do you believe these guys? They're so terrible, they got something wrong.'" But she thought that most of her viewers believed she was providing a valuable service by correcting any errors and that it also underscored the integrity of the show.

In addition to running corrections on the show, she was sensitive to how shaping the immense amount of data and news and facts and opinions that crossed her and her staff's desks each day, and the necessity to cite that information in a particular context, could piss people off.

In March 2009, she aired an edited, taped interview with *Left Behind* authors Jerry Jenkins and Tim LaHaye. Jenkins later complained that the edits portrayed them as fools and made fun of them, and he swore off any future taped interviews with hosts who held ideologically different views.

At first she was a bit defensive, but she soon came around to understanding his position. "I think we might have screwed that up," she said. "We should have told him, 'Okay, we are going to run this part of it.'"

She also worried that their very public complaint might scare off other Republicans from appearing on her show in the future.

"I am thankful for anybody who agrees to come on the show," she said. "I don't think personal animosity ever really enters into it even when I vehemently disagree with somebody. And particularly for people who disagree with me, I want them to feel like they have been treated fairly, like they haven't been ambushed, they weren't interrupted, and they had a chance to say their piece. And even if they don't feel like they came out looking great because the host disagreed with them, or they lost the argument or whatever it was, I don't want them to feel like it was an uncivil experience."

So she wanted to make it up to Jenkins and LaHaye. As her apology, she addressed the topic on her show and posted the unedited interview on the show's website so viewers could watch the segment in its entirety.

Despite the early accolades and transparency—and the fact that she could finally call the shots on a show of her own—Rachel had nagging doubts about whether she was on the right path. "I think I have a fear in general about whether being a pundit is a worthwhile thing to be," she admitted.

"I always feel like a fish out of water," she said. "Some of it is not having worked in TV before. Every host probably feels, 'I am not like those other guys.'"

She was also insecure about her on-camera performance. While she was already familiar with the grind of producing a live radio show five days a week, a nightly TV show was something else entirely, not only because of the visual aspect but also because of the pressure of serving a much larger national audience. "I don't know how to do TV right as far as talking to the camera, making sure the script's right, and doing good interviews," she admitted.

And though she had already faced the issue when she first started to appear on TV, she was still uncomfortable with the medium's emphasis on looks, usually to the exclusion of everything else, including content. "I dress like an eight-year-old with a credit card, and I eat like that too: burritos or pizza or s'mores," she admitted.

But she felt there was a danger in straying too far from what made her comfortable. "I don't actually think there's a reason to aim to be at the really high end of the prettiest people on television, because then you have to stay pretty the whole time you're on TV, and as soon as you stop being that pretty, you get taken off," she said. "I don't want you to be so distracted by the way I look that you can't focus on what I'm saying."

Despite this, she admitted it still bugged her. "I was very self-conscious about being visually presented, and I still am, to a certain extent."

But at the same time, she recognized that she had to accept certain conventions when it came to being on camera.

"I decided at the start of this that there are certain things that you need to do visually in order to be on TV, like you need to wear a blazer and you need to have makeup put on you," she said. "Then you don't have to think about it again. The not thinking about it is an active value for me."

As a visual artist, Susan knew how important presentation was—especially under the harsh lights of TV—so she stepped in to serve as an informal wardrobe consultant on occasion and suggested Rachel stick to a palette of gray, brown, or black to prevent the headlines from revolving around her wardrobe.

One on-air change she did have to make—reluctantly at first before going all in—was to wear contact lenses instead of her dark-framed chunky glasses, which created glaring reflections from the TV lights on the monitors. "It looks like they've got spangles on them," she said.

Continuing her subversive streak, she wore sneakers instead of shoes while sitting at the anchor desk. "That reminds me who I am, even though I am dressed up like an assistant principal," she said.

As her TV audience continued to grow, so did her radio listeners, as some fans couldn't get enough Rachel into their day.

And though she felt compelled to continue with her mission at Air America, she could maintain her insane work schedule for only a few months. In January 2009, the radio show shifted from the evening to five in the morning and morphed from all-original content into a rebroadcast of the MSNBC show from the night before, with Rachel offering up a few words as an introduction.

"I just couldn't keep doing both. I needed time to eat and sleep, which I wasn't [doing]. I needed to not be grabbing food off a cart at two in the morning," she said.

"I've been trying to simplify my life a little bit, because the TV show is hard. I've never had a job this good, and I still can't believe that I have it. But it's just wicked hard to do a good job in an hour of television every single day."

Though she was accustomed to occasionally being recognized by her voice when she was doing just her radio show, with the success of her TV show, she had to adjust to going out for a walk in Manhattan and having people approach her. "There's nothing all that fun about being recognized in the world," she said. "I don't get energy from people recognizing me and talking to me as a person they know from the media. If I could do my show in cartoon form where I didn't have to physically appear, I might enjoy that more because then I could have a more private life."

She also started to attract a fair number of persistent groupies, including straight men who'd ask, "Does it make me a lesbian if I have a crush on you?"

Rachel largely took it in stride. "It is a delicate balance between being very flattered by it and pretending it's not happening," she said. "I don't think it's helpful to dwell on that, because I don't think it can do anything good to my mind, [but I] appreciate that people are kind."

To Rachel, it came with the territory. "I mean, I am sort of detergent," she said. "I am a product."

She pondered devising a cover that would reduce the chances of being approached by fans when she went out in public. "I think I have to stop wearing my glasses on other people's TV shows because it's a great disguise," she said, adding that another consideration was to dress in a feminine manner. "In a frock, no one would know who I was."

And of course along with the fans came the naysayers and haters in the form of hate mail. "As a pseudo-public figure in the media, putting myself out there is the first refuge of scoundrels for attacks," she said. "Rather than say, 'Well, I really disagree with her position on Mitt Romney,' [it's] 'That dyke, I can't believe that she thinks she's even qualified to talk about an upstanding man like Mitt Romney.' It shapes the character of the personal attacks."

She accepted the threats, verbal abuse, and even death threats as part of the territory. "The only noticeable uptick that I get in kooky, I'm-gonna-get-you threats is when I do [stories] about conservative media personalities," she said. "It's when I'm talking about someone's favorite talk-show host, and that makes them want to kill me."

Most notably, they were fans of Glenn Beck. "He's telling his viewers that I'm a liar and a propagandist for pointing out his cockamamie claim that snowfall disproves global warming," she said on her February 16, 2010, show.

"Most homophobic stuff has a violent tone to it, like

'I'm going to kill you,'" she said. "I get that all the time. I purposely make it hard to contact me. I don't have a landline phone. I don't have an office phone. I don't open my own mail."

Rachel estimated that 10 to 15 percent of the population absolutely couldn't stand her. "They think I'm a man or a socialist and want me dead," she said. "Fortunately NBC security is really good. If you look out that window, you'll see snipers." It was unclear whether she was kidding or not.

She was also occasionally seen traveling with bodyguards and sounded a bit wistful for the olden days. "It used to be, I think, that we agreed on the basic facts that we were fighting over and we had different opinions about them. Now I think we accept different sources of authority."

Despite the threats, Rachel tried to remain optimistic not only about her future but about the future of others, particularly when it came to feminism. "Feminism is . . . by definition an oppositional movement, because it's trying to accomplish something," she said. "Everything about feminism is about getting something in the world to get better for women. I don't think of it as feminism versus anti-feminism; I think of it as feminism versus the world."

But the kudos definitely outweighed any negative reaction, because as if she didn't already have enough to do, in the wake of her newfound popularity, publishers came calling. But Random House beat the others to it; even before her TV show debuted, Rachel had signed a contract to write a book to investigate the effect that politics in all its guises has on all branches of the military in the United States.

Just how she was going to find the time to write the book was unclear, owing to her already packed schedule. "I have bad time-management skills," she admitted.

"I scramble all day, it is so unhealthy. I am going to be dead by the time I am forty. Of course, I have been this way my entire life, so maybe not. I am inured to it."

Then, exactly two months after her show debuted, another record was achieved when Barack Obama was elected president of the United States.

While Fox News and conservative radio hosts came out of the gate the day after the election with both guns blazing, chastened by their defeat, their Democratic and liberal counterparts on cable news cheered the historic election. But privately, many were concerned that they wouldn't have anything to write about now that their party was in power. Rachel had no such qualms.

"I don't think we are at risk of idiocy going out of fashion in Washington," she said.

She didn't, however, hide her admiration for the president-elect. "I like wonky in a politician," she said.

Though she is a vocal self-avowed liberal, she's admitted that she finds the Democratic Party to be boring and predictable compared with how the Republican Party operates. "It's fascinating how Republicans pick their candidates," she said. "Honestly, I think the Republican Party's voters are drunk. I'm sure they're having a great time and they feel euphoric, but you can't eat a ton of greasy food and not feel terrible in the morning."

CHAPTER 10

Off the Clock

As 2009 DAWNED, the overwhelming success of the previous year continued to be a constant threat when it came to Rachel's free time. Never good at managing her time, she established a routine where when she was in New York during the week, she went all-out with everything, but when she traveled home to Massachusetts for the weekend, she essentially turned into a slug.

"I'm a puddle of nothingness at home," she said, generally filling her weekends by mixing up cocktails, devouring her stack of graphic novels, and chopping wood. And sleeping and taking lots of showers, in addition to spending time with Susan. "I go to great lengths to turn the brain off."

And she jealously guards her time off. "I live what I think of as my own life between two A.M. Saturday morning and seven A.M. Monday morning. I get to see Susan, who is patient enough to put up with me."

One of their favorite weekend activities is to crank up the

local country music station and dance around in the living room until they become dizzy and collapse on the sofa, giggling.

They also spend time with Susan's family. In the intervening years since Rachel had come out to her family, her parents had eventually made peace with their daughter and also warmly welcomed Susan into the fold. "We all get along," Rachel marveled. "My family really likes Susan, and I think Susan's family likes me, [but then] Susan is more lovable than I am."

Rachel's lifelong propensity to have coherent, respectful conversations with people with differing opinions extended into her family life as well. "My sister-in-law, Susan's sister, is a lifelong NRA member and super wicked conservative, and her mom has Fox News on all day," she said.

And their house wouldn't be a home unless they had at least one dog, preferably two, and always male. "Susan thinks we are better with boy dogs, she's convinced we shouldn't have girl dogs," said Rachel, though she never was clear about the reason. "This is such an article of faith to her as to who we are as people and our relationship as pet owners, we talk about everything but we never talk about that. We just treat it as received gospel."

This "received gospel" also extended to the issue of when to neuter their dogs. "When we got our dog, the people we got him from warned us that he was going to be a big dog and that [we should] wait as long as we can before neutering him," she said. Of course, Rachel being Rachel, she wanted an explanation and asked, "Not to be weird, but don't you want those to be as small as possible when you cut them off?" They explained that keeping him intact would help his bones and muscular system to fully develop, which in turn would help to support his large body and reduce the chances of developing arthritis later. "We waited as long as possible, and Susan and I made a pact that we would neuter him as soon as he starts humping."

Always a big book reader, Rachel also spends chunks of each weekend reading everything from comic books and graphic novels to the latest political bestsellers, and reading is the one exception she made in keeping her work world from intruding on her free time. "I have to read a lot of new books fast in order to interview people and to know whatever is going on right now, and also if a book is changing something that is going on in the news," she said. But to her dismay, she found that her method of reading a book had totally changed. "I don't have a lot of time to read books outside of the stream, or any old books, so I only read new books now. I also read differently than I used to. One thing I look for in books is to . . . try to figure out why things happen."

When it comes to comics and graphic novels, Alison Bechdel's *Fun Home* and Greg Rucka's *Queen & Country* series are some of her favorites. "If graphic novels were in an orphanage and the orphanage were on fire, I'd rush in and save them," she said. And on her weekly commute between Massachusetts and Manhattan, she favors audiobooks. "In three and a half hours you can do a lot of trashy thrillers."

She also follows baseball, football, and basketball and doesn't neglect to hide her New England sports preferences when she's in Manhattan, openly flaunting her Red Sox cap, though she admits there is a downside: When she picks up a newspaper at the corner stand the clerk adds sales tax to her total on days when she wears the cap.

"I enjoy fighting with Yankees fans," she said. "It's cathartic for me."

With the occasional "Cocktail Moment" segments that she introduced as a lighthearted way to end her Friday shows, Rachel has made no secret that she is an ardent fan of alcoholic beverages, but not for the explicit purpose of getting drunk; instead, she regards the art of making a cocktail as a methodical yet nostalgic technique. She's more in love with the process than the end result. "I like making drinks even more than I like drinking them," she admitted.

She maintains a well-stocked, thoughtfully curated liquor cabinet at home and loves nothing more than to wander aimlessly through websites devoted to classic cocktails from the 1950s and 1960s and then lovingly make them for Susan and friends. "I don't drink any flavored spirits," she said. "If the ingredient existed in 1895, I'm interested in it. If not, I'm not."

She's so methodical in her bartending habits, in fact, that she admits she's incredibly slow. "Every recipe in my cocktail recipe repertoire starts with 'First, open a beer,'" she admitted. "I'm so slow, I need to provide refreshment to people who are waiting for me to produce a cocktail."

While she frowns on "mocktails" such as virgin piña coladas

and the like—"I don't believe in having cocktails without alcohol"—she isn't pushy about foisting her creations on people who are teetotalers or who otherwise abstain. "I am an alcohol enthusiast, but I am not an alcohol evangelist," she said. "I don't think that people who don't drink, should. But I think if you do drink, you should drink well."

And to Rachel, that means flavorful drinks that are not necessarily for the lightweights among us. "I like big drinks that aren't afraid of the alcohol in them. Not big in size, but in flavor, and the way I can allow myself to enjoy them is by making them in very small quantities. I make tiny glasses of very big drinks."

In her view, the biggest faux pas a drinker could commit would be to order a vodka martini. In fact, she frowns on using vodka at all. "I think vodka is for people who don't like alcohol, in which case, you probably shouldn't be drinking it."

Again, her propensity for big flavor rules the day. "If you think about the damage that you're doing to your liver by consuming alcohol, it ought to [at least] taste like something," she said. "The whole point of vodka is that it has no taste or smell. Okay, awesome, that's like going to an oxygen bar; I'm sorry, but I get that for free. There's a really good juniper-flavored vodka called *gin*, drink that instead. Vodka is a very good solvent for cleaning silverware and metal, and you can actually use it as a preservative in jams or simple syrup for making cocktails and stuff."

Even though she favors "tiny glasses of very big drinks," she'd be the first to admit that occasionally it can lead to some interesting decisions. After years of refusing to keep a TV in the house, Rachel broke down and ordered one from Amazon in 2009 after one too many cocktails.

"Susan and I ordered take-out Chinese and I made cocktails and somehow it just happened," she said. "Of course, since we were drunk, we had it shipped to the wrong place, so now we have to get this giant box all the way to New York City from Massachusetts and figure out how to install it since neither of us has had a TV in years and years."

She expected to watch some Red Sox games along with Patriots football games, but one thing she wouldn't be watching was other news shows, on MSNBC or elsewhere. "I don't watch other people who do the [same] kind of work that I do because I don't want to accidentally ape what other people are doing," she said.

But she didn't have much to worry about, since she turned the TV on only once. "I'm terrified of the television," she admitted. "I'm worried that I won't work, I won't eat, I won't sleep, I won't do anything, I'll just get sucked into it."

In 2009, as Rachel came up on the first anniversary of the show, she had a lot to be thankful for: She had her own show, she was controlling the shots, and if her schedule was a bit nuts, at least she had a chance to kick back and totally tune out on the weekends.

But most of all, she was thankful for Susan. "The best thing in my life is my relationship," she said.

With her growing fame, other women—and the occasional man—would sidle up to her and start flirting, but she admitted it didn't happen that often. "It's not like I'm hanging out in bars like I was when I was nineteen," she said. "One of the reasons I don't have much of a nightlife anymore is that if I'm in a crowded bar or restaurant and I'm talking really loud, I can't speak the next day, and it's hard to go out late night in Manhattan [to a place] that's not loud."

With everything going so smoothly in her life, some wondered why she and Susan hadn't tied the knot yet; after all, gay marriage had been legal in Massachusetts since 2004. But despite her success of the last year, Rachel still viewed herself as a perennial outsider, which naturally extended to marriage: It was just too mainstream for her to be comfortable with.

"I'm for marriage rights in terms of what I want the laws to be, but personally, in terms of how I culturally feel about my community and us losing something when we gain those marriage rights, I'm ambivalent," she admitted.

She also had qualms about the possibility that as her tribe assimilated it would lose its sense of community. "As gay people get more integrated into society and are less ghettoized, our lives will be just like everybody else's, and that's sad to me," she said.

"I'm a pro-subculture person. I love gay culture and I lament that so much of it is drawn from our need to survive discrimination and violence," she said. "I love that we are not mainstream and I love the right to get the rights the mainstream has. But I don't ever want it to make us normal."

She justified her concern on a creative level. "I worry that if everybody has access to the same institutions, that we lose the creativity of subcultures having to make it on their own. And I *like* gay culture."

In fact, a big part of her lamented how accepted gays have become in society, and she actually voiced regret about how easy it is to come out today and how open and easy-to-find the gay community is. "Gay culture is more normative today," she said. "It was really important as a kid coming out that there was a gay community with physical gay places in the world. Kids are coming out on Facebook now," she added with a bit of disdain.

Despite her own views, Rachel definitely advocated for gay marriage. "For me, it's kind of like the right to serve as a gay person in the military," she said. "I don't know whether I would want to do that, but I value military service. I also value marriage. If people want to do that, they damn well better have the right to."

She viewed it as a matter of equality, pure and simple. "If what you want is equal rights, you want equal rights," she continued. "And it's worth demanding equal rights. If somebody's telling you to wait for them, it's hard for them to argue that they're also on your side. If you're in the position of being an advocate, you're in the position of asking for what you think is rightfully yours."

But she wasn't a bit shy about admitting that she turned into a total mush at Gay Pride parades. "I love Gay Pride, [especially] the PFLAG contingent, where the parents walk past with the signs that say 'I love my gay son.' I don't cry, I dissolve. I'm a mess for an hour and can't do anything else and have to go home."

And she was not the least bit ambivalent about serving as a

role model for other gays and lesbians and actively encouraged others to come out whenever possible.

"Being closeted sucks," she said. "It means that you are in danger of being outed, and you have to keep track of shit that you shouldn't have to keep track of." Although she had very little experience living in the closet, she detested what it represented. "If you are closeted you have a secret, and if someone knows that secret they have power over you, and that is no fun."

She admitted that she had a clear advantage from being open about her sexuality from an early age. "When I look at people who are in my peer group who decided not to come out, the years that they lived closeted were bad years compared to how it was once they came out," she said.

"I'm never going to tell anybody when they should come out and when they shouldn't. Everybody needs to find their own way," she added.

"In general, people have to make their own call, but I think that a lot of times we overestimate how dangerous it would be to come out when really we're just nervous," she said.

"The single best thing about coming out of the closet is that nobody can insult you by telling you what you've just told them."

At the same time, Rachel made it clear she wouldn't hesitate about yanking someone out of the closet when he or she has been publicly homophobic. "I'm in favor of outing when people have demonized or scapegoated gay people for their own public gain," she said. "When they have risen to public prominence on the backs of the gay community that they are part of and they prey on, I think that's absolutely deserving of outing," she said, though under certain conditions. "I don't think just being a Republican or [expressing] mild personal hypocrisy or sneaking around is reason enough. [If you] have achieved your political office at least in part on the basis of your campaigning as a family-values paragon. I think it's community defense. It's one way gay people need to stand up for ourselves."

She maintains that coming out has far-reaching implications. "Coming out matters," she affirmed. "Coming out is powerful. It doesn't work only when saints come out. It's about seeing people as fully human entities and having to reckon with whatever it is you don't like about them in nonreductive human terms. That's the magic. That's how the moral arc of the universe bends toward justice."

In fact, Rachel viewed coming out as an almost mandatory move in order to provide inspiration to others who will follow. "There is one less secret in the world, and whoever comes after you is going to have an easier time," she said. "It's an ethical responsibility because people went before you and came out and that made it easier for you. And if you do not pay that back to the universe, the universe will kick your ass."

With hindsight, she regretted the way that she had come out to her parents. "I wish I had been more sensitive to [them]," she admitted. "But I certainly don't regret coming out. I think that everybody has to find their own way on coming-out issues, but not everybody has the option. When I was a freshman in college, I felt like I had the option, and I exercised it with an exclamation point. I think it says more about being seventeen than it does about being gay."

The longer Susan and Rachel were together as a couple, the more they thrived. Because Rachel was admittedly more one-dimensional in her interests, she came to rely on Susan's artistic sensibilities in broadening her horizons. "She cares about things other than politics, and I am kind of politics obsessed. . . . She's got adult interests that aren't politics, and so I do not deserve her," Rachel said.

She also adored the cute handkerchiefs that Susan gave her; Rachel particularly appreciated them since she had a tendency to become a bit misty and emotional on air. But they also served a valuable purpose when it came to feeding Rachel's vast array of superstitions: "A handkerchief can never be put in another pocket after it has been in one pocket," she said. "I don't walk under ladders. I have items of clothing that are lucky for me. That rotates, but I am luck oriented."

Perhaps it wasn't a surprise that Susan's career also benefited from Rachel's increased visibility. More important, her partner's fame—and the financial success that came with it—made it possible for Susan to give up the part-time bookkeeping jobs she'd been cobbling together for years, most recently for Mass Humanities, a local nonprofit organized to expand humanities programs at social programs throughout the state.

She'd always dreamed of being a full-time artist, but now that the chance had finally arrived, she hesitated about making the jump. Like Rachel, Susan had lived a fiercely independent life for years and was reluctant to give it up. They regularly discussed the issue, and Rachel finally encouraged her to take the leap, telling her, "It's about the fable you want to write about your own life."

So in early 2009, Susan took down her bookkeeping shingle and become a full-time artist. Indeed, her first year was a whirlwind success right out of the gate, with openings at galleries in New York, Provincetown, and San Francisco.

Like her partner, Susan is passionate about particular American traditions, and she possesses a strong patriotic streak, especially when it comes to the industrial buildings and structures she calls upon in her own work. "There is something really beautifully American and wonderful about these places," she said.

Her choice of medium reflected her sensibilities: She worked almost exclusively with Polaroid cameras and obviously expired film. "My whole art life changed when I discovered old Polaroid cameras and peel-apart film," she said.

In addition to working with the unpredictability of old film that is constantly changing because of age and climate—which helps contribute to the otherworldly sensibility that's present in much of her work—Susan has shunned techniques that many other photographers consider to be necessary tools in their arsenal: She refuses to crop her photos, she only enlarges them; doesn't like to use flash or other artificial light; and eschews the use of Photoshop or other software programs to tinker with the end result.

Her photographs captured a bygone era through a gauzy filter. For one 2010 show, *American Device: Recent Photographs*, she traveled along the coasts of California and Texas to photograph oil refineries and ports because she was struck by how beautiful they appeared to her, a view that she admitted might be difficult for other people to grasp.

"For all of our great high-tech industries, places like this . . . are still a part of the lifeblood of our country and our culture," she said. "But there's also no denying that in many ways they're increasingly at odds with our modern times. And that conflict is part of the poignancy that makes them so beautiful to me."

The filter through which Susan views the subjects she chooses to pursue in her art is oddly similar to how Rachel views the world, able to see the positive and negative in everyone. "This is how America works," she said. "This is how people make their livings and raise their families, and that's always been an important part of these industrial sites—but there's the downside to them, too."

Susan's career started to take off as exhibitions of her work began to appear in galleries across the country, as well as locally in the Berkshires. After focusing on photographing abandoned symbols of the Industrial Revolution, she created a new exhibit entitled *Photo Book*, where she focused on delving into stories based on compelling images that captured her imagination when she was a girl, particularly those that originated in children's books about a girl who took control for herself.

She continued to work with her beloved Polaroids, which represented a couple of uniquely American traditions: "I love, love my Polaroids," she said. "To me they are the very beginning of America's complete love affair with the instantaneous."

Like her longtime partner, Susan appreciated how as the technology became more affordable, it spread to people who previously couldn't afford it. "[Polaroids] were a great democratization of photography," she said. "It was the second time that photography was made available to ordinary people."

But she was totally at the mercy of the sheer volatility of the expired film. "Aged instant film doesn't just produce weird colors: it's also unpredictable," critic and author Christopher Bonanos explained. "When [Susan] goes out to shoot, she might have a hundred and twenty frames' worth of scavenged old film in her bag, and if thirty of them don't work—as is entirely possible—her day can be severely curtailed."

But that's part of the reason she loved it. "Colors drop out from old film, and red is the first to go," she said, which is why she used newer film from 2007 to 2009, since she wanted to capture lush reddish colors for the exhibit. She also shot the photos only in the afternoon, the time of day when it's possible to capture reddish tints from the sun. "It's like squeezing the color out of a sponge," she said.

Susan was well aware that the cameras and especially the film were becoming rarer by the day, and as a result she was already planning for the future, when she could no longer purchase Polaroid film from eBay and garage sales. So she decided instead of moving forward and using modern-day photographic techniques, she'd go in the opposite direction and work with tintype photography and pinhole cameras, two early forms of photography. "It's a crazy plan to go backward in time, not forward!" she admitted.

Aside from working with "old" technologies—Susan with her Polaroids and Rachel spreading paper out on the floor of her office before she writes—she and Rachel have one thing in common when it comes to their work: They both take their time to ensure that it comes out right, with Susan admitting that she works very slowly when it comes to her art. She not only conceptualizes an image in the early stages, but also which technique and camera would work best to enhance the final product. She also places special emphasis on how the idea conjures up specific emotions and memories for her. So while she might marinate on a future work of art for days, weeks even, since all the groundwork is set down, taking the actual photo can occur in a matter of seconds.

Rachel was thrilled that Susan was finally able to pursue her dreams. "I'm so proud of her," she said, adding that while her own TV success was gratifying, she'd give it all up in a second if that's what their relationship needed.

"And if it made sense that I needed to stop being on TV and go live full-time in the Upper Peninsula in Michigan and raise chickens, we'd go live in the Upper Peninsula and raise chickens. It's the single clearest thing in my life."

CHAPTER 11

Behind the Scenes

IF YOU'VE EVER seen any snippets of Rachel as she prepared for her show to go live, most often the last two minutes before airtime involve a camera capturing her from behind as she mad-dashes down the hall, pulling on one of her numerous dark-hued jackets, occasionally struggling with a sleeve, followed by an all-out sprint to the set, where she leaps into the anchor chair with maybe a second to spare before the "ON AIR" light comes on, the opening graphics dance across the screen, and she says, "Good evening," a hint of breathlessness evident in her first words. The show is a runaway train and Rachel is the superhuman engineer veering and gaining speed throughout the day, trying to keep the wheels on the rails.

"Every day, it's a shock [when nine o'clock arrives] and the show's only ninety percent done," she said.

"Doing the show is like jumping out of an airplane. Here it

comes, it's nine o'clock. This is going to happen no matter what I do."

An hour later, she signs off and after a post-show scrimmage with her core staff, she heads out of the studio to grab a late-night bite and cocktail at Daddy-O, a nearby bistro that serves food until four o'clock in the morning.

Everything that must occur in order to get that "ninety percent done" fifty-three-minute-long show on the air and Rachel flying into her anchor chair five nights a week is an exquisite and painstaking—and painful—superhuman rush of consuming the day's news, stirring it up, and then serving it up so that it's palatable on the other end, assisted by staffers who do everything from clearing permissions for old news clips and pre-interviewing potential guests to blocking out the camera angles over the course of the show.

"Rachel works incredibly hard, but it takes a village every night to get it on the air," said executive producer Cory Gnazzo.

"Rachel is a one-woman data-mining operation," said Kent Jones, who worked with Rachel on her radio show and continued on to the TV show.

The entire process is in service to Rachel's number one thesis of the show, the concept that every story idea must go through before making it onto the air: To introduce viewers to a story that hasn't been overplayed in the rest of the mainstream media while also not getting too cerebral—or negative.

At times, it is a precarious balancing act. "First, we need

to be able to synthesize a lot of information, and then exclude from our field of consideration the stuff that isn't important so we can find the salient, new thing," said Rachel. "And that is very rarely something overt."

Before she heads out to the studio, she starts her day in quiet, waking up around eight o'clock. "I'm not a morning person," she admitted. "Before noon, all I'm capable of is marmalade and mumbling."

And she tries to avoid the media as much as possible; after all, she'll get plenty of it in just a few short hours. "I usually don't spend too much time looking at the news before I come into the office because I try to compartmentalize my life a little bit, so I have a little bit of sanity, a little bit of usable brain by the time I get to work," she said.

Sometimes she goes for a run, a sport that she picked up only when she was thirty-eight, despite the fact that she was an avid competitive athlete all throughout high school. However, her favorite sport has always been fishing. She finds it relaxing, allowing her mind to wander before heading uptown to the studio. Sometimes she even drops a line in the nearby Hudson River in the wee hours of the morning to de-stress after the show wraps.

Before she arrives at the office around noon, Rachel gears up for the day by reading a lengthy note prepared by a senior producer that spells out what she and other top staffers anticipate the biggest stories of the day will be and why they think they should make it onto the show a painfully short nine hours later.

Rachel also scrolls through her own news sources, marks up the likely candidates, and then climbs into a car that will ferry her a couple of miles away to midtown and the MSNBC studios at 30 Rockefeller Plaza.

Before she opens the door, Rachel takes a few deep breaths in the car. They're the last few normal, unhurried breaths she'll have for the next ten hours.

Her first task of the day is to hole up in her office for the next two hours to comb through her list of story ideas along with the morning note from the producer. Then she prints out all of the competing story ideas from a variety of websites and spreads them out all over her office. "I get down on the floor with all my paper, and I make this big grid which is very embarrassing," she said.

She admits that her process is neither efficient nor green. "I am a paper monster," she said, going through about five hundred sheets of paper to print out newspaper stories, journal articles, and copy pages from books so she can scrawl all over them and arrange them in some semblance of order.

What does she consume? Basically a little bit of everything.

"I have my must-reads: *The Wall Street Journal, The Washington Post, The New York Times, National Review,* though we try to geographically change up the sources of information, so I also try to read the *St. Louis Dispatch,* the *Texas Tribune,* and the *Portland Press Herald* on a rotating basis, particularly if I know something interesting is happening in that state," she said. "That's also fun, because that's where you get the little giblets of stuff that people don't necessarily know about . . . and we can introduce [it]."

From there she gets a little wonky. "*Government Executive* has some stuff in it that will lead down some interesting paths, and there are some bloggers that I love on water policy and people I trust who blog on voting rights."

She also relies on several staffers who have wonky specialties of their own. "I've got one guy on my staff who's really good on energy issues, another who's good on the Middle East, and somebody else who is a little OCD about states you've never heard of, like [the fact that] Nebraska has a unicameral legislature."

But no matter what she reads, she tries to avoid reading the opinion pages of any publication, focusing only on originally reported stories and editorial content. "I don't want to absorb other people's opinions and I don't want to become part of a tide of common wisdom on something, I'd rather be my own thing," she said.

"Much more than I wish was true, I tend to at least subconsciously agree with the last thing I heard that made sense, and so I try to consume as much fact and reporting as I can and as little of other people's analysis as I can."

During this phase, she has to shut the world out because she's afraid she might miss one little nugget that would make the story absolutely shine. "The best part of the story might be a very small detail," she said.

"You follow the storytelling. If you can do good work or you can add something that is truly not known, people might watch it, even if it's on something very obscure. And the more obscure the topic, the better the storytelling has to be."

She adds that unlike other hosts, she never underestimates the intelligence of her audience, and she tries to talk to her viewers the same way she would if she were leading a seminar in graduate school. "I do think if you are good enough at expository writing and the use of visual elements, you can get to an incredibly intense level of detail, and have people really get it," she said. "But you have to be good at it."

Through the years, some of her staffers have told her to ease up, that she doesn't have to spend every afternoon as though she's cramming for the hardest finals in the world. But she ignores them, because she is motivated by just one thing: fear of failure.

"It's not that I believe a segment will be better because I read those extra twenty pages, it's because I'm worried that if I don't, I'll say something wrong," she admitted. "It's negative motivation, which makes for a high-stress atmosphere."

Two hours later, she knows that she's barely scratched the surface, but with airtime a mere seven hours away, the next phase of the schedule kicks in: Twenty senior producers and staffers gather with Rachel in a cramped office, where they duke it out on a big whiteboard over the stories and guests that will make it onto the air that evening. Rachel writes down a working headline for each story she'd like to do, based on a combination of the morning news notes and news she's already reviewed, while staffers call out their own ideas of what should be covered that night.

Sometimes their ideas will be miles apart, and the tension in the room will grow thick, but over the course of the next hour, a list of roughly fifty different story ideas will somehow be whittled down to just six.

"I ask questions, cross some things out, and add my own stuff," said Rachel. "I usually add as much as [my staff], then we hash it out in terms of what seem like the most important stories of the day. It's a very hard discussion, and we try to go fast, because time is of the essence at that point, but we work it out."

They put the most likely ideas under a microscope, analyzing the angles and arc for each story, considering a list of possible guests who could come on the show on very short notice, hypothesizing how the competition may be covering the same topic that night, and pondering how the story will evolve in the hours before airtime. It's a lot to digest.

As she scrawls ideas and rationalizations onto the board, often ferociously underlining them to drive home her point, Rachel might be mistaken for a college professor defending her ideas and arguments for the topics she believes deserve coverage that night, albeit one dressed in a brown hoodie, jeans, and a Boston Celtics T-shirt.

Frequently, she becomes so passionate about making her argument on the whiteboard that staff members have to ask her to decipher her handwriting. "There's usually a direct relationship between the legibility of my penmanship and my level of confidence in the segments," she admitted.

"By the end of the meeting, I've usually changed my mind," she said. "It's a grumpy meeting. A little testy."

And she occasionally second-guesses the choices. "Every time you cover one thing it means you can't spend that time covering something else," she said.

But despite the fact that staffers—and Rachel—often leave the meeting feeling as if they've just participated in a cage fight, everyone involved maintains that the scrum and emotions running high are worth it. "It's the best part of the day, the most intellectually satisfying part of the day," said Rachel. "If I ever had to give up this job, that's the thing that I know I would miss."

Her preference is unusual in the business; on other shows, staffers will decide on the stories for the day as well as their formats—straight news story, "A-block," or guest interview?—before meeting with the producers, a small group who will then meet with the host to finalize the show. "I am the final arbiter of what goes on my show, but that doesn't mean that I don't take advice," she said. "I need advice all the time, and that's why we meet as a group, that's part of the reason why I do my news meeting every day. I like to meet with everybody because I want to get lots of people's input. I also sometimes go randomly to staffers and ask, 'Between these two stories, what do you like?'"

After the meeting adjourns at three o'clock, they all head off to their own turf to write, research, edit, and gather materials for the six segments they finally agreed upon. "I close the door and turn off the lights and turn into sort of a cave-dwelling beast for as long as I can and just read and read and read and read and read while the producers are reading and collecting evidence and calling people and reporting and doing what needs to be done."

Her office is a testament to the chaotic pig-through-a-python superhuman process of putting together an hour-long show from scratch five nights a week. Stacks of paper cover desk and floor, crammed manila folders in stacks threaten to keel over, water bottles are strewn here and there, and stray Diet Dr Pepper cans perched on bookshelves share space with books such as *Debunking 9/11 Myths* and *The One Percent Doctrine*. Phil Griffin might have been overly diplomatic in describing her office as something akin to a library, while Rachel takes a more pragmatic view: "This is how I'm going to die one day, crushed under a pile of paper," she said.

She starts by outlining and jotting down notes for "A-block," her monologue that opens the show, for which she does most of the writing, sometimes with a boost from Laura Conaway or another staffer. "A lot with that opening essay is me working it out with the producer, us agreeing on the universe of facts and evidence that we're going to use and then talking through it while a producer records what I say, and then he or she types it up, and then we work out an edit together based on what I said."

Other staff members work on developing the visual graphics and illustrations to accompany the stories, including maps, which Rachel detests. "Maps are the bane of my existence, because it's impossible to do mapping on television for some reason," she said. "Everything always looks like it was made with a freaking Etch A Sketch, it's a 1970s Atari pixelated nightmare, I hate it, so we start working on maps early."

Depending on how much time is left until airtime, Rachel tries to meet with each of the producers in charge of the other segments for that night's show. "It's a combination of us writing together, [a producer] writing something and bringing it to me, me writing either just directly into the script software that we've got, or sometimes me dictating," she said.

But no matter what stories are scheduled for that night, or how many producers are on deck, Rachel admits that her propensity toward putting off the writing—whether for "A-block" or a later segment—is "a broken process. I should start writing at four thirty, but sometimes I don't start writing until six thirty."

She admits that it not only turns her into a ball of stress, but that it negatively affects the people who work with her. "It's reckless. It kills my poor staff. They're so supportive and constructive. But it's too much to ask. [The show] requires everybody to do everything fast, and if I could just get it done an hour earlier, I think I would put ten years back in the lives of all the people who work with me."

The last stretch is indeed harrowing, with staffers alternating between frantically running around trying to get everything done and sitting eerily quiet, focused intently on putting the final pieces of the puzzle together as the minutes tick by until 8:46 P.M., which is the absolute witching hour when Rachel runs to the makeup room. "I give them eight minutes to make me up," she said.

She then runs from the makeup room to her rack of similarly hued jackets, grabs one seemingly at random, then sprints to the set and jumps into the anchor chair. "I arrive like fifteen seconds before the show starts," she said. "It's an incredibly, incredibly stupid system. Nobody else's is that disorganized. But it works."

Even after the show goes live, Rachel and her staff are still alert to new developments and breaking stories that could throw the carefully planned show schedule into disarray and require her to basically improvise on camera as a new story develops.

For example, just thirty minutes into the April 25, 2018, show, Rachel announced that they had received word of breaking news from Reuters about Ronny Jackson, President Donald Trump's controversial nomination as secretary of the Department of Veterans Affairs, and staff scrambled to get Leo Shane, the deputy editor from *Military Times*, to appear on the show on very short notice to comment.

On the other side of the coin, guest bookings are a frequent casualty due to a news cycle that could change on a dime. "[Booking guests] never works out because I always change my mind at four in the afternoon," she admitted. "I send people a lot of bottles of wine and apologies for unbooking them."

On the other hand, there are many people who don't even pick up the phone when they see who's on the other end. "I don't think you go on *The Rachel Maddow Show* without doing a lot of preparation," said Phil Griffin. "You cannot wing it. She's going to be smart, and she's going to ask hard questions."

After years of working by herself—on her academic coursework, thesis, and radio show—Rachel found it difficult to adjust to the team-mentality attitude that putting a live hour-long show on the air requires.

"Occasionally, I will just throw the segment producer's work out and write the whole thing myself," she admitted, causing great dismay to those who have put their all into crafting a segment. "It's unfortunate, but it happens."

At the same time, she acknowledged that she wouldn't be where she is today without them. "I have to rely on other people to help me tell the story that I'm telling, so I need to be able to count on not only the people who provide me with the facts that go with the charts that I'm putting on the air, but also the people who are running the videotape and putting up the captions and labeling the people," she said. "I'm completely mystified by [it]."

Once the "ON AIR" light goes on, an eerie peace settles over the studio, and it's by Rachel's design: She doesn't want to think about the fact that almost two million people are focused on her every word, along with countless others who will catch snippets of the show on social media.

She also doesn't want to be distracted by any superfluous motion or talk in the studio that could distract her from the task at hand, so she limits staffers to just two: her floor director and the guy who operates the jib camera, which resembles a seesaw, with a camera on one end and the controls on the other. Sometimes Susan will stop by, but that's it. "I pretend no one can see me when I do the show," she said.

"I need to trick myself into thinking that I don't have an audience, because I need to be focused on the stories that I'm telling," she said. "If the camera is turned on you, you [start to] think of yourself as an influential person, and that can build up an evil ego and also mean that you are not thinking all that clearly about your subject matter because you're so focused on yourself and the world.

"And if you start thinking about what effect you're gonna have on the world, I think it makes you pull your punches. Or it makes you slant things in a way where you're trying to move the world in a specific way."

Sometimes she thinks of her mom during the broadcast, especially when she feels herself getting worked up during a particular segment. "Every once in a while, I can't stop myself and I get a little all caps, and the person who reins me in on that is my mom," she said. "She's violently attuned to loud, so I get a nice little note from my mom—'You're raising your voice'—

and she calls me afterward so I can hear in her voice how serious it is."

The chaos is restricted to the control room in 2K, located one floor directly beneath where Rachel perches at her desk, and it's in that control room where techs and producers are entrusted with making sure the right visuals appear on screen to accompany Rachel's words at the precise time—so that the wrong button doesn't get pushed and the "Cocktail Moment" graphic shows up instead of "You Know More Now."

Or worse. On October 18, 2013, instead of "Cocktail Moment: HEIST EDITION!" part of the graphic was cut off the screen and viewers saw "Cock Mom HEIST!" over Rachel's shoulder as she smiled and raised her glass in a toast, unaware of the screwup.

Bianca Shea got a firsthand look at that on-air chaos when she interned at the show in the summer of 2016. She often had to conduct detailed fact-checking or search online for relevant videos or graphics whenever breaking news hit while the show was live. "One night, I was in the control room when they needed something pulled off the internet for a tape producer so it could go on the show in fifteen minutes," she said. "I ran across the building and up a flight of stairs, downloaded it, and emailed the producer the video code." The video made it onto the show with just seconds to spare, which tends to be the modus operandi at the show.

When the show breaks for a commercial, instead of taking advantage of the respite to kick back for a couple of minutes or make small talk with others, Rachel turns to her computer, typing notes to herself for one of the upcoming segments or perhaps for the following day's show.

Or maybe she thought of a more nuanced way to convey a bit of information for an upcoming story. After all, she does consider herself to be first and foremost a storyteller. So in addition to providing her audience with the facts necessary to round out their understanding of a story, she has to be concerned with exactly *how* she tells that story, the degree of emotion, empathy, and humor.

And to Rachel, there will never be enough time for that. "I think an overt part of storytelling [is] to think about the emotional content of what you're doing, and that has two parts," she said. "One is your tone of voice, how much emotion you show and whether or not you are upset about something, [because] if you are raising your voice, people will hear less of what you are saying. [Instead], be persuasive, be authoritative, and have a voice that people can listen to.

"I am as rage filled as the next guy," she admitted, though she rarely allows it to flash on camera. The same can't be said when she is covering a story of a prominent politician's downfall brought on by his or her own incompetence, greed, or stupidity; in those cases, it's almost impossible for her to hide her joy. "I defy anybody to have shown more glee or spent more minutes of airtime enjoying the spectacularly corrupt and profane downfall of Rod Blagojevich in Illinois," she said. "That stuff is gold."

In fact, just as there's never enough time during the day to produce the perfect show that night, there's also no time during the show to cut loose, it's so highly scripted. Kent Jones, for one, would love to improvise a bit on air, even make Rachel laugh at something unexpected. But he admits that Rachel's penchant for writing out every word she utters on the air, plus the fact that they are never able to squeeze in everything they would like to, means that Rachel dropping the mask for even a few seconds is a rare occurrence. "We don't have enough time," said Jones. "We were on the radio together for years, and you can stretch out a little bit on the radio, let a moment happen, but [on TV] we don't have time to let go, as much fun as it would be to do."

One of Rachel's pet peeves, on and off the air, is when someone ends a sentence with an inflection that makes them sound as though they're asking a question; she thinks they "don't sound authoritative."

In fact, she hates it so much that she forbids her staff from putting a question mark in anything they write for her, even when a segment requires Rachel to ask a question of a guest. "There will never be a question mark used as punctuation in any script ever given to me," she said, admitting that she's struggled with this very issue. "But it's a worse problem [for millennials]. You have to cut that shit out. Really. It's very serious. I have not hired people who talk that way, because I know that I can never, ever use them on camera."

She also tries to keep the emotion out of her voice whenever she's on the air because she doesn't want viewers to think she's trying to manipulate them, though she admits that this is sometimes difficult to achieve. "We [often] cover things that are outrageous that get [viewers] worked up, but *I* should not be outraged when telling the story," she said. "Instead, I should be focused on creating that feeling in the people who are watching, don't tell people I'm upset or angry, *make* them upset or angry. I have to block myself off from the audience in a way so that I'm doing a good job but I don't tell people how I feel."

She also tries to hold a little bit of her personality back, so as not to reveal everything, and keep a little bit of the real Rachel in reserve. "When something moves me, I pay attention to my own feelings, stick a pin in that, and then try to make sure that gets into our broadcast about the show. So, it's very personal, but it does mean I have to kind of show myself a little bit."

Once the show wraps, she heads back to the makeup chair to scrub off the foundation and mascara, meets with a few staffers to assess the show, then heads out sometime between ten thirty and twelve thirty to a neighborhood bistro to grab dinner and drinks, sometimes with a producer or two in tow to discuss future shows. But one topic of conversation that is rarely broached at these post-work gatherings is how the most recent show went, because they already know how Rachel feels about it: The vast majority of the time, she's unhappy with how it unfolded. "I see my job as making a TV show, and I fail at it constantly," she said, admitting that on most shows she gives herself a C grade or less, due to technical challenges, less-than-scintillating guests, as well as her own skills as an interviewer, which she pegs as subpar.

In fact, she has occasionally tortured herself after what she perceives to be a particularly wretched show by telling herself that she just did such a lousy job that she's convinced she's going to be fired the next day. And if the show ever went off the air, what would be her greatest loss? "My freedom," she said.

She's not hard on herself all the time, of course; whenever she thinks the show went well, undoubtedly it's because she feels she's been able to deepen people's understanding of a particular story and make them see it in a new light.

But for the most part, she also tries to ignore feedback on how a particular show or segment or the program overall affects her standing and fame in the world. "I don't know very much about how I am received in the world in the sense that I don't know how people see me or use what I do because I purposely isolate myself from it," she admitted. "I don't feel like that would help me be better at it, and I feel like it might weird me out."

But she relished whenever public figures attempted to further their profile by poking fun at her. "Wow, [former United States senator] David Vitter thinks that he's going to get somewhere that he isn't already by talking about the fact that he thinks I'm too masculine? It's a great compliment."

Even though Rachel considers herself to be a lone wolf when it comes to the bulk of the work she does on her show, she worries about the effect that the relentless pace of cranking out her show has on her staff. "I think about all of these brilliant young producers who work on my show, and essentially working on my show is the process of grinding your bones to dust each day, an inch at a time," she said.

"Six segments, new content, new angle, something fresh, five days a week, fifty weeks a year. And keeping the energy level and staying focused even when you're not moved by anything going on in the news is hard. You need a facile enough brain to have that many interesting things to say about that many different subjects that many times a week, week after week after week," she admitted.

"It's hard to keep people for the long haul."

Admittedly, not everyone is cut out for the brutal pace. By the same token, not everyone is able to deal with Rachel as boss, calling all of the shots. She confided that whenever a newly hired producer believed that she would be able to steer the course not only of an individual show or segment—instead of Rachel—that the staffer's tenure would not last long.

The fact that Rachel was not particularly fast at any aspect of her work—except when it came to talking—only added to her workload and pressure. "I'm a very slow worker, it takes me a really long time to do anything. I'm like a little sloth, the way I get through stuff, and so I work very long, plodding days," she said.

"It takes me a good solid ten hours to prep an hour of TV, and that's with not taking a lunch break and not making any phone calls and not talking to anybody about anything other than the show that day, and not reading my emails."

Despite her track record, she does hold out hope that someday it will get easier. "I assume that I will get better at this and not take so long to get everything done, in which case I'll have some more time [to do other things]."

CHAPTER 12

Branching Out

As Rachel's fame was on the upswing, the opposite was happening at Air America. By early 2010, even though their rebroadcasts of her show from the previous night were garnering decent ratings, the challenges facing the progressive radio network finally proved to be too much. The company filed for Chapter 7 bankruptcy in January 2010 and ceased operations owing to its financial struggles, specifically the challenge of selling advertising as the Great Recession became more entrenched, as well as the fact that most programs aired on smaller stations with less of a geographic reach.

Some believed that the odds were against the network from the beginning because of its mission and audience. "Conservative or regressive radio has an easier time of it because what it does is tap into [people's] lesser nature," said Janeane Garofalo, who had hosted a show on Air America until 2006. "It's really easy to do that. That's why it has the success it has:

because it allows assholes to think they're doing good things, to think they're patriots. Working for radio that speaks truth to power, that asks people to be better, to be good citizens, to participate in democracy, is not as easy as what regressive radio does, which is ask people to do nothing."

Indeed, people who listen to conservative talk radio typically skew older and whiter and live in more rural areas where only a few stations may be available. By contrast, the Air America demographic was not only more urban but also younger and more racially diverse. They were also more inclined to listen to their own self-selected playlists on their newfangled iPods and iPhones than on a tinny AM car radio.

Rachel, for one, took it in stride. "Air America made a good run of it for more than five years in a very challenging climate," she said. "The modern iteration of talk radio evolved as an almost entirely right-wing phenomenon. Air America tried to change that and did succeed in shaking up the format a bit. It also recognized and developed a lot of great progressive media talent who have gone on to a lot of other gigs."

Including, of course, herself. Besides, her own show was keeping her more than busy. And in the meantime, MSNBC was in the process of reinventing itself as a bastion of progressive news as well as a place for highly intelligent viewers who could appreciate—and expect—both nuance and subtlety. "I'm not saying we're NPR, but there is an appetite for really smart discussion of the news," said Bill Wolff.

At the same time, Rachel made it clear that she didn't regard

MSNBC as strictly liberal while maintaining that Fox News was 100 percent conservative. "I think that's a caricature of us . . . but I don't think it's a fair caricature," she said, claiming that MSNBC brings more "nuance" to its presentation and is "more unpredictable."

As the ratings for *TRMS* soared, accolades continued to pour in from places large and small. In October 2009, *Esquire* magazine named her one of "The 75 Best People in the World"—a list that included Lyle Lovett, Shepard Smith, and Beyoncé—singling Rachel out as "a whip-smart voice of reason in the racket that is cable news."

And in 2010 she made *Forbes*'s "World's 100 Most Powerful Women" list.

Rachel was honored but nonplussed and largely deflected the credit to MSNBC, saying that it was her producers who "encouraged me to be quirky and opinionated, and not to be like everything else on TV. It's hard for me to know why someone watches me," she added. "My influence extends only as far as between me and the camera. I'm not trying to change things, I'm trying to cover them."

To someone with such a broad reach and avid fan base, her reticence and hard-line self-criticism reflected her discomfort with being in the public eye, especially since she wasn't a huge fan of TV in the first place, and considered the medium to be valuable only if it managed to increase the amount of useful information in the world. She admitted that being on a TV show where millions of people were watching her each night was not only a highly stressful situation, but also quite unnerving since she was previously accustomed to imagining significantly smaller audiences on the other end.

Despite becoming such a recognizable celebrity, she wasn't comfortable being in the spotlight. "I feel lucky to have all this attention and all of these people wanting to talk to me about what I'm doing," she said. "The only hesitation I have is that I'm not interested in media about media. I feel like I sometimes struggle to be interesting in talking about how I got here."

She also had an issue as she started to be regarded as a brand by the network and fans. "And what's weird about cable is that people get really engaged with news hosts as brands. I don't want to insert myself into the story. I just want to give a useful analysis of it to help people come to their own conclusions."

So while previously she agreed to every magazine interview, college talk, or appearance at a trade show, Rachel increasingly began to turn down more of these requests. For one, she simply didn't have the time, but she also wanted to feel less exposed. "I've become better at saying no, because I'm protecting what I'm doing more," she said.

"My agent [Jean Sage of Napoli Management Group] has a standing order from me: If I am asked to do something that is not my TV show, the answer is no."

Of course, she's known for not always taking her own advice. She did occasionally take advantage of fun, frothy things, including a cameo on *Ugly Betty* in 2009; and when George

Clooney asked her to appear as a news anchor in his 2011 film, *The Ides of March*, she couldn't say no.

"My agent was like 'George Clooney called. I know, it's no,'" said Rachel. "And I was like 'Oh really, George Clooney? It's really hard to say no to him.' So there I am, I'm a Hollywood sucker. I'll do anything for George Clooney."

But otherwise, because she didn't watch TV and she read mostly for work, Rachel pretty much lived in a cave when it came to anything involving culture or the arts, and she regularly drew a blank when staffers mentioned a currently hot star or even if she was actually standing next to one.

"I'm so pop culture illiterate that I did not know there was a connection between Bruce Jenner and the Kardashians," she admitted. "It also took me a long time to figure out that the Kardashians don't have jobs."

NBC launched *Late Night with Jimmy Fallon* about six months after Rachel's show, which resulted in an awkward elevator moment where he said hi and she said hi and then they both acted like anyone does in an elevator, watching the numbers creep by, looking at the floor, and generally avoiding small talk even though they obviously knew who the other was.

Her ignorance about popular culture—along with her determination that her appearance be the least important thing about her show—was particularly ironic when she discovered that both male and female fans started to dress like her. "I think that is inadvertently hilarious, which is my favorite kind of funny," she said. "My whole idea about what I wear on TV is that I want it *not* to be the thing that you notice about what's happening on TV at that moment."

But even back in 2009, fashion experts were not surprised at the growing prevalence of stylish lesbians in the public eye. "People are realizing this is about rethinking how lesbians are adopting fashion, with makeup, great haircuts, tailored clothes, about finding a new take," said Hal Rubenstein, fashion director of *InStyle* magazine. "There is a certain kind of androgynous sensuality that both Maddow and [Ellen] DeGeneres possess that men and women, gay and straight, find very appealing."

Lesbian comedian Kate Clinton agreed. "Rachel is so clear, so funny, but also, she is herself, and that is what's really sexy to people," she said. "What we're doing with butch and femme is playing around with stereotypes. She's dead serious, but there's a real sense of play in what she does."

"My gaydar used to be better," Rachel admitted. "Now I feel like every [woman] who is fashionable seems gay to me."

At the same time, while some of her hard-core fans from the early days might rue her new mainstream image, Rachel pointed to her racks of $19 dark jackets from H&M as proof that she hadn't strayed far from her roots, though in addition to those cheap jackets, her on- and off-camera wardrobe also featured a few high-end pieces from Jil Sander and $300 eyeglasses from MOSCOT NEBB, along with Converse's Chuck Taylor shoes. Plus, "I wear just as much makeup as the other guys on MSNBC," she quipped.

But never jewelry. Always cognizant of the buzz that she'd

create if she changed some aspect of her wardrobe even a tiny bit, she refused to wear any jewelry while on camera, saying that she didn't want to spark any speculation among eagle-eyed viewers who would interpret any external change as proof of an internal one.

"It takes me about fifteen seconds to get dressed, 'cause I only dress from the waist up." Hidden by the anchor desk are jeans and her Chuck Taylors. "It's like a mullet: it's business upstairs, party downstairs," she joked.

"I'm a lesbian who looks like a man, and that's *on purpose*," she affirmed. "It's not like I'm trying to look some other way and I'm messing up. This is it. This is actually the way I want to look, and [as for] the whole 'OH MY GOD you look like a dude! I know how you could be pretty!' Guess what? I don't want to."

Two years after the show launched, it was going through its own growing pains. For one, while Rachel's ratings in the first year of her show coincided with the 2008 presidential election season, the show's ratings over the following year had dropped precipitously, which is not an uncommon occurrence as TV news networks gain a bit of breathing room and discover there are other topics to cover besides politics. Nightly viewership of *TRMS* in March 2009 averaged around 1.1 million people, but by late 2009, that figure had fallen to just under nine hundred thousand a night.

Rachel was not concerned about the decline, at least not publicly. "We don't debate the ratings very much," she said. "My main concern is keeping the quality of the show high."

Even though guests were not the prime focus of the show, as her reputation for asking hard-hitting questions in interviews grew, fewer people wanted to appear on the show; some didn't want to be challenged and couldn't stand up under the glare of her white-hot questioning, whether they were liberal or conservative.

"I could get more people who disagreed with me on the show before than I can now, and that is disappointing because I hoped that by modeling civil discourse and by not ambushing anybody, that might be a way that people who disagreed with me would want to engage with me," she said. "That upsets me because I don't like to talk to people who are like myself so much, I enjoy talking to people with whom I disagree. I learn from them, and if my own arguments are missing something. If I have a confrontational feeling toward somebody who I think is really doing something wrong for the country, it is much more satisfying to me to explain that to that person rather than just rant to a TV camera about it." She did acknowledge that there is an inherent risk she also faces whenever she invites an adversary onto the show. "Anytime I invite anybody on my show who doesn't agree with me, there's a risk that they're going to show me up on my own program."

But it could also be that Rachel was becoming increasingly difficult to pin down. Even though she is a self-described liberal, she has never been shy about acknowledging some commonality with the other side, which especially in this day and age could rattle conservatives and liberals alike, making them more reluctant to accept a guest spot on the show.

"What motivates me is much more pedestrian than what motivates most lefties," she said. "I'm motivated by the Bill of Rights, by equality and injustice issues. In today's politics, that makes me a lefty. I'm a GI Bill American; if someone proposed the GI Bill today, they would be run out of the country on a rail as a socialist."

Along those lines, some of her gay fans started to grumble that her show wasn't gay enough and, more pointedly, that she didn't come down hard enough on people with virulently antigay attitudes. Asking Mike Huckabee his views on gay issues wasn't exactly news, in Rachel's eyes; besides, it didn't satisfy her credo that anything that made it onto her show had to add something new to the conversation.

"I weighed whether or not to ask him about his antigay views, but I really don't care about them very much," she said. "I also probably wouldn't bother asking Sarah Palin about her antigay views if I had the opportunity to interview her."

Many in the gay media disagreed with her philosophy. "That was pretty jaw-dropping," wrote critic Michelangelo Signorile. "The problem with having someone as dangerous as Mike Huckabee on your show and giving him a pass on these issues is that it gives him another opportunity to put a smiley-face mask over his ugly evangelical conservatism."

"You'd be happier if I was doing a sort of a gay rights show," she said in a written response to Signorile, adding that her take on her interview with Huckabee was strictly from a news-oriented perspective, while she underscored that any criticism of the degree of gayness on her show is totally beside the point. "I can't do the show as a non-gay person, I don't have that option."

At the same time, she maintained that it was important for hosts to draw from their backgrounds and use their own life lessons to help them convey their opinions and beliefs to viewers. For instance, her years of working on behalf of people with AIDS has clearly influenced her thinking and actions. "I learned that people should speak for themselves, and that manifests on my show . . . in that I do long introductions before I let guests talk but the payoff is that they get to talk without being interrupted," she said.

"But I think it's pretty hard for animals to figure out how we became the animals we are," she added, just as she regarded her lifelong depression and its tendency to pop up in her life at odd moments that she cannot predict. So just as she became open about discussing how her sexuality influenced her news judgment—or not—for the first time she started to publicly acknowledge her cyclical depression, as she thought it might help others who were struggling with psychological issues.

"It was a hard call because it is nobody's business," she said. "But it had been helpful to me to learn about the people who were surviving, were leading good lives, even though they were dealing with depression. So I felt it was a bit of a responsibility to pay that back."

Aside from a couple of sessions when she was in her twenties, Rachel did not find meeting with a therapist to be helpful. "Talking about myself for an hour, it's not something that I would pay for the privilege of. It just sounds like no fun."

Instead, she waits it out. "The way I experience depression is a real closing off from the world," she said.

Her self-criticism also intensifies. "One of the manifestations of depression for me is that I lose my will and my ability to focus," she said.

"It's like somebody hits the mute button. It's very lonely, and it can be alienating," she admitted.

"The time when it's hardest is when I have forgotten that this happens to me and so I don't know what it is," she said. That's when Susan steps in and basically sits Rachel down and tells her point-blank: *You are depressed.*

"She reminds me that I'm having an episode and that it's temporary and I shouldn't allow it to stop my life," said Rachel.

"I can't make the depression go away, but I can be cognizant of it. It's lifesaving to me that Susan both knows about it and understands it and pays attention to me on those grounds. As I've gotten older, the exact cyclical experience of it in terms of how long it lasts and how frequently it comes changes a little, and I just try to be patient with myself. If it ever becomes permanent, I'll need to treat it medically, but right now I don't," she said.

Apparently, goofy pictures help somewhat. When she feels really down in the dumps, she calls upon a photo of the late John McCain wearing a tie that looks as though it belongs on a clown.

During her depressive states she might lose her focus, but she never loses her perfectionistic tendencies and her never-ending belief that her show can always be better, although she has learned when to pull back. One time, the show's guest booker arranged for three authors—including activist filmmaker Michael Moore and former president Jimmy Carter—to appear at separate times over the course of one week in 2011. But Rachel insisted on cutting the appearances down to two.

"Rachel said, 'We have to postpone Michael Moore because I can't read three books this weekend, I can only read two,'" said Bill Wolff. "Michael said, 'Nobody reads the book!' But Maddow totally reads the book."

With almost two years of in-studio shows under her belt, Rachel was getting a bit restless with the format of the show; it also felt a bit too safe to her. So in the summer of 2010, she and a group of producers and camera crew headed for Baghdad to report on the end of Operation Iraqi Freedom, as U.S. combat troops and thousands of contract employees were starting to leave the country. The show broadcast from Baghdad for a full week amid scorching temperatures, sporadic electricity, and undrinkable water.

Rachel was absolutely in her element, later describing that the work she did in Iraq was "some of the best reporting I've ever done in my life." The highlight was seeing areas of the city that were rarely visited by media and interviewing local families and sharing a meal with them, even though her visit was during Ramadan, when Muslims don't eat or drink water from sunrise until sunset.

In contrast, when she had gone to Kabul, Afghanistan, the previous month, her work was curtailed because she was required to embed with the U.S. military, which discouraged her from speaking with locals.

In both cases, the logistics of broadcasting live were challenging, involving technical issues and simply getting from one place to another and making sure they had everything they needed to produce the show, despite the constant threat of bad weather and older technology preventing the production team from operating as smoothly as in the New York studio.

But in working on the other side of the globe, she worried about losing her objectivity and honoring the show's mission of putting more useful information out into the world. "When you are really out of your element, in an environment that is completely new, it is hard to keep track of your own editorial voice, and not reflect back some of the novelty where it is that you are," she admitted.

But her worry was for naught: The two-day live Afghanistan broadcast—"Good Morning, Landlocked Central Asia"—

won the Emmy Award for Outstanding News Discussion and Analysis.

Being away from the studio—albeit in a war zone—emboldened her to broaden her horizons. While she was in Baghdad, she wrote a song with a longtime Massachusetts friend, the singer Erin McKeown, via text. McKeown had asked Rachel to appear with her at an upcoming benefit for birds injured by the *Deepwater Horizon* oil spill in the Gulf of Mexico in 2010.

"We ended up, by text message, via some dodgy satellite connection, writing the lyrics to that song that ended up at the benefit for the birds, so it's about birds and oil and Baghdad," said Rachel.

McKeown debuted the blues-inflected song "Baghdad to the Bayou" at the benefit for the World Wildlife Fund at the Town Hall in New York and selected it for her 2013 album, *Manifestra*.

Rachel was on a roll; despite the tight time constraints of her show, she was eager to take on even more projects outside of her regular show responsibilities. Her next venture was to write an introduction for a graphic novel featuring Batwoman. *Batwoman: Elegy*, by Greg Rucka and J. H. Williams III, was published in 2010.

Plus, she checked one dream off her bucket list when she appeared as herself on an episode of *The Simpsons*, trying to figure out why Kent Brockman—the cartoon news anchor on the show—is so envious of her. She introduced the clip on her show and was nearly jumping out of her seat. "It's the best thing in my life, *ever*," she said. "I will never achieve anything this cool ever again in my life."

Reading between the lines, one could argue that all this extracurricular activity served either as a warm-up to finishing her first book, *Drift*, which was actually contracted for before *The Rachel Maddow Show* launched on MSNBC in the fall of 2008. Perhaps to placate her editors, she publicly downplayed these side projects in the media.

"I work really long days," she said. "I'm really happy doing what I'm doing and I'm not looking to do something else on top of what I'm doing. I'm not trying to pick up extra work."

And yet she was doing just that.

In early 2010, Massachusetts Republican senator Scott Brown floated a rumor that Rachel was planning to run against him as the Democratic candidate in the upcoming 2012 Senate race. He sent out a fund-raising letter to rally support and she immediately took out a full-page ad in *The Boston Globe* accusing him of using fearmongering tactics to raise money for his campaign.

"I never said I was running against Scott Brown. The Massachusetts Democratic Party never asked me to run against Scott Brown. It's just not true. Honestly. I swear."

While she tended to get misty-eyed at the idea of the Bill of Rights *Schoolhouse Rock!* style, she wasn't particularly enamored of the system as a whole. "I love politics, but I think that our constitutional democracy is a terrible and corrupt system," she said. "While I think that being a member of Congress is one of the most honorable things that an American citizen can choose to do . . . I think most of the people who do it are scoundrels."

It was clear that Rachel had mixed feelings about living the public life of a celebrity. She occasionally became wistful for the old days of Air America, even for her salad days when she started out at WRNX. "I miss local radio, that sense of being part of a community," she admitted. "It was a really potent way to learn the power of radio, and the responsibility of it, you're not some voice of authority and power somewhere, you're a person talking into people's ears. There's no filter. People feel like they get to know you, so you ought to be worth knowing."

But the financial rewards of being MSNBC's star meant that she and Susan could finally move out of their closet-sized Manhattan studio and buy a place where they could spread out. In June 2010, they paid $1.25 million for a 1,325-square-foot apartment in Greenwich Village at the Harbor House, 130 Jane Street, which had served as a paper warehouse from the time it was built in 1898 until the mid-1970s, when it was converted into apartments. The apartment's previous owner was Michael Stipe, the lead singer of the band R.E.M.

After a real estate blog ran a story about the purchase—which included a picture of the actual floor plan—Rachel was furious that the piece included her specific address, railing against the site's decision to include the information as clickbait without considering how it would affect her life to have complete strangers—and enemies—show up on her doorstep. "Whoever decided the actual address and floor plan was necessary to get those page views, I hope they die in a fire," she said.

In 2011, MSNBC renewed Rachel's contract.

No surprise there; her ratings had rebounded by 34 percent in February from a year earlier, along with a 19 percent jump in viewership just since January. In retrospect it came as no surprise, because on January 21, Keith Olbermann announced that he was leaving not only *Countdown* but MSNBC as well, as of that evening, shocking fans as well as advertisers who had committed to buying airtime months into the future.

To those who were closely following the inner workings of MSNBC, the abrupt end of the show wasn't as out of the blue as it seemed. Two months earlier, the network had suspended Olbermann for making campaign contributions in 2010 to Representative Gabrielle Giffords and several other Democratic candidates, which was a direct violation of network regulations. Staffers behind the scenes also pointed to the fact that Comcast was in negotiations to buy NBC Universal—which included all of NBC, plus their news division, along with MSNBC—and rumor had it that once the purchase was complete, Comcast would have a heavier hand in dictating the direction of news tone and programming at the cable network.

Countdown was replaced the following week with *The Last Word with Lawrence O'Donnell*, which was moved from its ten

P.M. slot to serve as a lead-in for Rachel. But the ratings for O'Donnell's show were sluggish; *Countdown* viewers were dissatisfied with Olbermann's replacement and perhaps to protest his departure skipped the show entirely in order to focus on Rachel, which resulted in that month's boost in ratings.

Shortly after he left, Olbermann signed on with a project at Current TV, a new cable network funded partly by former vice president Al Gore that was promoted as an even more progressive alternative to MSNBC. Olbermann resurrected *Countdown* at the new network and then started to drop hints that he was trying to convince Rachel to join him.

MSNBC obviously didn't want to take any chances of losing another star, so they renegotiated Rachel's contract a full year before her current contract was due to expire and significantly increased her salary, up from the $2 million she had been making.

"Rachel is our quarterback," said Phil Griffin.

After the deal was signed, Rachel went on the record that she wasn't going anywhere. "There isn't any other job in TV that I want," she said, affirming her commitment—but not before her chronic insecurity leaked out. "My big goal is to finally do this right. Someday I'm going to do the show I want to do."

In the end, it's a good thing that Rachel stayed put: A little over a year after Olbermann left MSNBC, Current TV fired him for breach of contract; Olbermann then sued Current TV, arguing that it was the network that had violated the contract, accusing it of not giving him enough control over his show. The matter was resolved out of court.

With her new contract settled, Rachel could turn her attention to promoting *Drift*, which she had finally finished in 2011. Her long-awaited book was published on March 27, 2012.

Even with an avid worldwide fan base and complete freedom to cover anything she wanted for a full hour five nights a week, fifty weeks out of the year, Rachel still felt there wasn't enough time to say everything she wanted to say about many subjects, but particularly when it came to the military and America's involvement in wars over the centuries.

"The issue of how we decide about using military force and starting and ending wars has been bugging me for essentially a decade, and I felt like the short form of the media that I work in wasn't allowing me to say exactly what I meant, it's more of a long-form idea," she explained.

"I'm really bothered by the fact that we have been at war for ten years, since 9/11, without most of the country noticing that we are at war. War is supposed to be very dislocating for the American people, it's supposed to be hard for us to go to war."

While many of her critics on the Far Right might have been surprised at an outspoken lesbian with progressive views writing a coherent, intelligently argued book about the politics of war, Rachel made a point in interviews to spotlight the fact that she came from a military family and that her father was an

Air Force captain. "A lot of members of my family have served, and if it had been legal for openly gay people to serve in the military at the time I might have been considering signing up. I think service is honorable, and that was always inculcated in me," she said.

"I am not a pacifist. I have a lot of respect for pacifism, and I do not share the belief that war is always the single, worst option."

Drift hit the top spot for hardcover nonfiction on the *New York Times* Best Seller list the first week it was out—where it remained for another month—while *Kirkus Reviews* named it one of the best nonfiction books of 2012. *Los Angeles Times* critic David Horsey was impressed. "Her book very much reflects the way she comports herself on TV," he wrote. "And, far from being a left-wing screed, it presents a sharply argued commentary that many conservatives could buy into."

As was the case when she broadcast her show live from Iraq and Afghanistan, Rachel looked forward to going on a book tour and clearly relished the opportunity to meet and talk with people face-to-face. She spent a full month on the road, mostly sticking to the East and West Coasts, with her only Midwest appearances in Milwaukee and Kansas City. As a bonus, Susan went along on the tour.

At the lectures and talks that accompanied the bookstore appearances and signings, she was able to really dig into the niggling little details of the issue as well as explain her own motivations behind wanting to explore the topic in greater detail to people on both sides of the issue. "I'm a civilian who didn't go [to war] and who feels alienated from the people who went in my name," she admitted. "I'm really trying to [explore] the emotional feeling of disconnect between us as a country and the people who have been fighting these wars. If we don't feel sacrifice while we are asking people to make increasing sacrifices, that is both unfair and unsustainable."

Though many members of the military were interested in what she had to say, Rachel affirmed that she really wrote the book for people like her. "I wrote *Drift* for a civilian audience, for an America at war that doesn't feel it," she said.

And she looked forward to the opportunity to meet fans and readers of all ages. She was particularly surprised that so many younger readers came out to cheer her on. "There are a lot more kids in the Model UN than you think," Susan quipped after the tour was over.

Rachel agreed. "There were all these moms who would come up to me and say, 'Do more "Moment of Geek"—my kid loves it!'" she said.

There were also lighthearted moments. At a talk in Milwaukee, someone asked, "What cocktail goes best with *Drift*?"

"A French 75," Rachel quipped, using the term for a French weapon but also drawing on her extensive cocktail research for the drink of the same name. She then proceeded to spell out the ingredients for the recipe: gin, syrup, and lemon juice.

CHAPTER 13

Settling In

In the four years since *The Rachel Maddow Show* had gone on the air, higher-ups at the cable network began to apply Rachel's special sauce not only to other shows already on the roster, but also to the development and design of forthcoming shows—and, indeed, to help them pick which new talking heads should come on board.

Her format and tone proved to be so successful that it couldn't help spilling over into the rest of MSNBC's lineup, which added shows hosted by Chris Hayes, a progressive white journalist—who had subbed for Rachel when she was in Afghanistan in addition to other times—and Melissa Harris-Perry, an African American journalist and professor.

"I admire what Rachel has done and I absolutely would not be doing this if it weren't for her," said Hayes. "What she is able to do in prime time is remarkable. She has opened up a door on a whole new realm of possibility of ways you can create an audience."

Even in the wake of the departure of Keith Olbermann and *Countdown*, the new strategy worked. By the end of 2012, MSNBC had more than doubled its viewer audience in the 25–54 age bracket over the previous year, and *TRMS* had increased its viewership by 72 percent overall and by 111 percent in the coveted 25–54 demographic.

Even with such impressive figures, the network wanted to shake things up even more. Surprisingly, the topic of how Rachel dressed on camera was still coming up on a regular basis, both among network executives and fans.

One idea that was being bandied about was for Rachel to wear her everyday clothes—brown hoodie and T-shirt—but she quickly squelched that idea. "I would look dumb," she said.

"I want [my dress] to be essentially respectful, neutral, not distracting. If I could wear the same thing every day without that becoming a story, I would do that, and so I essentially wear a variation on the same thing every day mostly to create kind of a neutral visual experience."

Perhaps it wasn't a surprise, but as her viewership grew, people who might have turned down an invitation to appear on the show in the past now eagerly accepted, not only because of the increased exposure, but also because Rachel had proven her propensity to treat her guests with respect.

"If I've brought somebody into the discussion, it's because

I believe they are worth hearing, not necessarily because they always agree with me but because they have something to say that's going to advance our understanding of [what] I've been trying to explain on TV," she said. "It's counterproductive for me to bring somebody onto the show and say you're not worth listening to, or you're a waste of space, or I wish you didn't exist."

"I feel like I'm advising my viewers that this person has passed my test and that they are worth listening to," she said. "Feeding Christians to the lions is fun, too, but I want my viewers to feel like if I'm bringing somebody on, it's because they have something that is worth hearing."

She didn't often invite artists or musicians onto the show. "It's just because I'm a policy dork," she said. "I really like talking about policy and politics. It's hard for me to make broadcasting out of [arts and humanities], so I'm always a little reluctant."

She also refrained from inviting people she liked onto the show. "I think interviewing people you personally like is dangerous because you end up trying to make them feel better about the interview rather than getting something out of them," she said.

Her dream interview—still unfulfilled as of 2019—was former vice president Dick Cheney, to whom she dedicated *Drift*:

"To former vice president Dick Cheney. *Oh, please let me interview you.*"

"I think about [interviewing him] every day," she said. "He has answered almost nothing about the most controversial decisions he made, and I would like to try to get answers from him. His role in national security has become the stuff of legend, not the stuff of record."

She particularly wanted to delve into his inner workings and how he was able to convince people at all levels of power to do his bidding. "I don't find Cheney scary," she said. "Everyone thinks of him as a mastermind, but he's just a guy with bad ideas and bad execution of them. Dick Cheney gets far too much credit than he deserves."

On the other hand, there were people she would never ask onto the show even if the exchange would make for record-breaking television ratings. Rachel's litmus test for inviting guests is whether the person has something to offer to help her listeners. "Ann Coulter would not meet that requirement," she said.

That said, occasionally she will butt heads with a guest, or she or the guest will realize their on-air matchup was a huge mistake. In that event, she backs off and tries to block out the world; and sometimes staffers will help out. "When I get overwhelmed or frustrated on the TV show set, [producer] Kent Jones does a really funny turkey noise that makes me happy every time."

While she admits that the respectful approach that she takes toward guests with opposing views is responsible for building her career, she realizes that her method does have its limits. "The commentary industry on the right makes zillionaires out of these people, which gives them tons of incentive to be outrageous and provocative," she said. "Rush Limbaugh is really washed up at this point as a radio host, he's been around too long and he says too many of the same things. But every once in a while, he makes a calculated decision to say something to get himself in trouble, a little cry for attention. Everybody's outraged, people pay attention to him for another week, then he disappears again.

"And if you tell people, 'Don't listen to anybody else, you can trust only me, and everybody else is out to get you,' you get them to listen to you exclusively. That's how Fox News is so dominant in cable news. It's not that a majority of the country watches it. It's just that it has locked up all the conservative audience."

She refuses to change her approach. "Anger is like sugar in a cocktail," she added. "I'd rather have none at all than a grain too much."

Though she was never much for socializing in New York once her long workday was over, Rachel also made a decision not to hang out with or otherwise fraternize with people who make it into stories aired on the show. For one, even though MSNBC expected its star hosts to attend the White House Correspondents' Association dinner as a matter of course, Rachel refused. "I think it's weird to have dinner with people you cover," she admitted.

But they insisted, so they struck a compromise: She wouldn't attend the dinner, but she'd bartend at the MSNBC after-party. So at the 2012 event at the Italian embassy in Washington,

D.C., when she was in the middle of shaking martinis and peeling lemons, Greta Van Susteren from Fox News approached her and said she had to speak with her right away.

"I'm working here, Greta. Sorry."

"No, I need to talk to you," she yelled above the booming dance music.

Rachel started to turn away, but Greta took hold of her arm and dragged her across the room. "You need to meet somebody," she insisted, holding Rachel's arm out for a handshake, and suddenly it was shaking another hand.

"I looked at the hand, and looked up the arm, and [saw] it was attached to Sarah Palin," said Rachel.

The very Sarah Palin whom Rachel had once referred to on her show as "a prevaricating, mendacious truth stretcher or whatever other thesaurus words we can come up with for lying, is just far less efficient than calling a lie a lie, and a liar a liar."

"She was as deer in the headlights as I was, but I said, 'It's very nice to meet you.'"

"What are you doing here?" asked Palin.

"I'm bartending." They chatted a bit and Rachel was impressed by her genial demeanor before asking what she was drinking.

"Oh, you can't get me a drink."

"No, really. I'm bartending."

"Diet Coke."

"Lemon or lime?"

"Lemon."

As Rachel handed her a Diet Coke with lemon, she invited Palin on the show.

"I'll think about it," she replied, and went back to her corner and Rachel went back to her bartending.

The following Monday, she returned to the five-day-a-week grind, and the 2012 presidential election season heated things up even more. But it turned out to be a good thing for *TRMS*, as more viewers tuned in to see Rachel than Sean Hannity on Fox for the first time since her show debuted.

To her staff, the recognition was extremely gratifying. "She's able to process all the information and put it together in a way that makes people focus on what's really important," said executive producer Cory Gnazzo.

And while the churn and long hours of producing the show had a tendency to chew up and spit out some staffers who couldn't handle the grind, Rachel's respect for telling the story made others extremely loyal.

She also had a habit that comes in handy in the middle of a crazed newsroom when the minutes toward airtime are ticking down. "The more tense the situation, the more calm I tend to become—my breathing slows down and I relax," she said. "Once everything's settled, I'll get anxious, but only then. I don't know why it happens that way; maybe my adrenaline pump was just installed backward."

The constant stress was difficult on Rachel and wreaked havoc on her health, but she was careful about her health in at least two ways: She steers clear of sugar and most days tries to exercise, which she says she loves.

In addition to taking up running, she took her first boxing lesson the day after she turned forty.

After Barack Obama was elected to his second term in office, ratings took a dip, not only for Rachel's show but for MSNBC as a whole, a normal part of the news and election cycle. And while some thought a second Democratic presidential term would cut down on the number of topics considered for *TRMS*, Rachel said that had never been a problem for her. "Wouldn't it be amazing if the problem in news was trying to figure out what to talk about?" she pondered. "That's never been an issue for me. There have probably been only three days where I've felt like I was reaching, and that's usually because I'm hungover."

Her relationship with Susan remained as strong as ever, despite the groupies and fans who regularly interrupted a meal out or a simple stroll down the street to walk the dog. Rachel continued her routine of twelve- and fourteen-hour days during the week and retreating to rural life on the weekends; it was the only way she could keep up with the frantic pace required by her show. "I arrive in Massachusetts around two A.M. Saturday, and wake up so that I can put the trash and recycling together and get it to the dump, which closes at eleven A.M. Me and the dog go to the dump, then we drive to a sheep farm and I let the dog look at the sheep."

They also tackled a few home-remodeling projects in Massachusetts, including adding another bathroom since the original one presented physical difficulties, including a steep set of stairs. "Also, the house is symmetrical and historically preserved," she said, "and the idea that we would stick something onto it as an addition felt like putting a hat on a horse."

So they decided to build a one-room bathhouse a short walk from the house out in the woods, adding not only a second bathroom but a hot tub, fireplace, and big-screen TV. Rachel soon came to regard it as her private escape from the world, so that the extra bathroom was somehow beside the point. "I can seal myself in the bathhouse and watch football really loudly," she said.

It was her own version of a real-life desert island, perhaps spurred on by an interviewer who once asked her what she'd take to a real desert island if she had to pick "one food, one drink, and one feminist" to bring with her: "The feminist is easy," she said. "I'd take my girlfriend because I would be useless on a desert island. She's totally MacGyver, she can make a nuclear bomb out of a match and a palm frond. I would bring some sort of mezze platter, because I love to have a lot of different things so I wouldn't get bored. And for drink, I would bring Scotch . . . Susan doesn't like Scotch, so I'd bring Cuban rum—we both like that."

For better or worse, Susan has learned to adapt to the many strangers who email her with both positive and negative comments on her artwork specifically because of her relationship with Rachel. And though a few have offered up uncomplimentary feedback about her often out-of-focus work, even going so far as to suggest that she should see an optometrist, Susan has charitably welcomed all feedback.

They both received frequent requests from the media to talk more about their relationship—in both the public eye and private—and although Rachel knew that many gay men and lesbians viewed her as a role model, the topic of her relationship with Susan was mostly off-limits.

"There's a lot about my relationship with Susan that we just keep to ourselves," she said.

She did, however, offer up this tidbit: "I haven't felt alone in the world—I haven't felt *lonely*—in the thirteen years since I laid eyes on her," she said.

Though she does have a penchant for spreading paper across the floor of her office—something few other people at the show do—Rachel maintains that she is a true child of the internet and is an avid fan of wandering the web aimlessly to find funny cat and dog videos. "It's not a stretch for me to incorporate that stuff," she admitted.

After all, she was online years before the internet went mainstream: She wrote her honors thesis at Stanford in 1993 primarily by conducting her research online with a poky dial-up connection and the LexisNexis database, which was the main source for academic research at the time. "I'm a creature of the online world," she admitted. In fact, today she refuses to read anything in print except for books and obscure trade journals; the printouts strewn across her office floor are from websites and blogs that she regularly reads.

Her love of everything online also extends to giving credit where credit is due, making it a point to tell viewers where she originally read a story, whether it's *The New York Times* or a small-town weekly newspaper in Kansas. "I really am a believer in the cult of the reporter," she said. "We need reporting like a mammal needs blood. Being able to name resources and where they come from is an honor . . . and draws attention to the people who are doing good work."

As was the case on her radio show, Rachel continued to operate in an unorthodox fashion, not toeing any political line, but being open to anyone and any viewpoint as long as it helped to fulfill the mission of the show.

She confides that she probably relies on more Republicans for background than Democrats, though she's dismayed that they typically turn down her invitations to appear on her show. "I am buoyed by the fact that there are Republicans who have just seen me on TV and think, 'You know what, I could have a fruitful conversation with her that might help her understand the Republican world a little bit better.'"

Of course, like the rest of us, Rachel readily admitted to the dark side of spending hours each day online, especially on social media, which appealed to her nature because it evened the playing field for all kinds of people, but she struggled with it even as she benefited.

"We try to use our online presence not to just broadcast in a different medium, but to get feedback and information for the show," she said. "But because it's such a democratic medium, and because everyone has access to everyone else's first drafts and raw responses along with the more polished work, the process of reading and sifting blurs the lines between work and distraction. It sucks you in!"

CHAPTER 14

The 2016 Elections and What's Next for Rachel

As the 2016 presidential campaign started to heat up—though some might argue that the election cycle never really stopped—Rachel was gearing up for another intense season.

But just as she had started to branch out into other areas that were a little more free-form than her tightly scripted show she began to take on additional gigs that required her to loosen up and to rely on other people, some of which resembled promotional events of a sort.

In December 2015 she appeared in Flint, Michigan, to moderate a town hall forum on the city's water crisis. She had already devoted numerous stories on the show to the topic, but by becoming involved in the issue through holding city officials accountable face-to-face and on live TV, she was returning to her activist days, if just a little bit.

Then in early 2016, right before the Iowa caucuses and the New Hampshire primary, Rachel came on board for MSNBC's expanded election news desk, where she'd serve as coanchor alongside Brian Williams. She was also invited to moderate one of the prime-time Democratic debates among Hillary Clinton, Bernie Sanders, and Martin O'Malley.

Instead of being consumed by dread over the prospect of working without the net of a finely honed script, Rachel relished the opportunity, particularly because there was no clear front-runner on the Democratic side from the outset. "Nobody knows who's going to win!" she exclaimed. "I mean, who on the Democratic side knows who's going to win? That's freaking spectacular, just in terms of suspense."

But one aspect of her show carried over to her new gigs, where Rachel made no secret of her propensity not to criticize people who held opposite beliefs from hers. "I don't believe that people who disagree in American politics are all that different from one another as humans," she said. "No matter how much we disagree on a political issue, the one thing that brings us together is that we both care about a political issue. I like people who care enough to have an opinion."

And she didn't leave her humor far behind: "We've watched Jeb Bush set fire to tens of millions of dollars and get in trouble every time he opens his mouth. At one point he actually said, 'You are *looking* at the nominee and I am *going* to face Hillary Clinton and I am *going* to whoop her.' Come on, Jeb, you actually have to drop a *g* somewhere if you're gonna talk like an everyday person. You have to use a contraction."

Like other media professionals, she kept a close eye on Donald Trump and was alternately amused and horrified by his candidacy. "Donald Trump gets all his information from watching clips of people talking about him," she said.

And like others in the media, she and her producers increasingly tailored her show around the fact that she—and about half the population—couldn't believe that he was being backed so vociferously. "First of all, anybody in day-to-day political coverage who says they saw it coming you can write off for the rest of their life," she said. "To go from being a race-baiting nativist buffoon reality-star professional sexist to being the distant front-runner for the Republican presidential nomination, even for a while, says almost less about Trump than about the Republican Party."

In the late spring of 2016, as the show was coming up on its eighth anniversary, MSNBC decided that Studio 3A needed a little freshening up, both in appearance and in tech developments, so the show temporarily moved to another studio—6E—at 30 Rock, though astute viewers wouldn't have noticed anything different, since the set designers replicated the exact look of Rachel's home with still photographs of the old set. When they returned to the revamped studio in late August, there were new oversize LED walls designed to increase the resolution of the graphics that flashed behind her.

Rachel had just settled into her new space in time for the final frenzy of the 2016 presidential election when tragedy struck late in the evening of October 25: A three-alarm fire consumed the floors above Rachel and Susan's West Village apartment, creating extensive water and smoke damage and rendering their home uninhabitable for the foreseeable future.

Fire investigators discovered the cause to be in an electrical connection between floors, and the entire building remained unoccupied for a full year after the fire owing to extensive mold that had developed in the walls, along with built-up soot in the building-wide HVAC system.

They lost most of their belongings and had to move into a furnished sublet with their dogs, who were not injured in the blaze.

The next night, Rachel went on the air with no mention of the tragedy from the night before.

Less than two weeks after they were displaced, Rachel faced another shake-up when Donald Trump was elected president of the United States.

Unlike her colleagues at MSNBC and other news broadcasters who leaned toward the liberal, Rachel remained levelheaded throughout the night, although a right-wing website had released a doctored tape that showed a clip from earlier in the show when Rachel became emotional and ran it as a current news story, announcing that she had cried on election night after receiving the news of Trump's victory.

"I had no feelings on election night because there's a lot to do," she said. "I'm not a good ad-libber, and anchoring election night is five, six, seven, eight hours of ad-libbing, which for me is like juggling seven tennis balls while merging onto the freeway at night in the rain with no wipers and no lights."

When reality set in the next morning, she allowed herself some time for the news to sink in, but not for long, because after all, there was a show to put out. She fully realized that work would be a balm to help ease the shock of the election—even a tiny bit—because if she allowed herself to wallow in her despair and rage it would be that much harder to fulfill the central mission of the show: to increase the amount of useful information in the world.

But even before the inauguration she realized that she and her staff would be treading in uncharted waters. "I don't get weirded out by that much stuff in the news, but this puts a shiver down my spine: Our president-elect is lying to us."

Right after Inauguration Day, Rachel admitted that she felt as if she had entered the twilight zone. "After we cover the story that the president is saying things that are not true, the White House spokesman says stuff that is not true, then puts out written statements that are not true, then they [offer] people who in live interviews say things that are not true, and will not correct things when they are confronted about the fact that they're not true," she said.

As she tried to make sense of this new world order, one benefit was that more viewers were tuning in so they could make sense of things as well. By May 2017, her nightly audience averaged more than 2.3 million viewers, up from 849,000 in 2014.

And despite her bone-deep exhaustion, Rachel felt rejuvenated at the challenge of covering the Trump administration on her show. "I'm more energized about my job now than I have been in a very long time," she said.

"I see my job as explaining stuff, and boy, there's a lot to explain."

When the tweet came on March 14, 2017, at exactly 7:36 P.M., pandemonium broke out across the political spectrum.

Rachel Maddow MSNBC @maddow BREAKING: We've got Trump tax returns. Tonight, 9pm ET. MSNBC. (Seriously).

All hell broke loose in the Twitterverse and elsewhere as publications rushed to post the news online. MSNBC fanned the flames by posting a clock during the *All In with Chris Hayes* show, counting down the seconds until nine P.M., when Rachel would finally reveal the truth about the president's tax returns.

Fans—and detractors—on Twitter went nuts with the wait; journalist Mathew Ingram pointed out that "regular denizens of the Twitter media-sphere have the patience of someone sitting on a hot stove."

The frenzy made Rachel and her producers think that maybe they were overselling the story a bit. So to clarify, she tweeted again about thirty-five minutes before the show went on the air:

What we've got is from 2005 . . . the President's 1040 form . . . details to come tonight 9PM ET, MSNBC.

When the familiar theme song came on and Rachel appeared on screen, viewers were on the edge of their seats. Where were the returns? "In just a second, we are going to show you exactly what it is we've got," she said.

She then spent a full twenty-two minutes providing background on why it was so important to finally get a look at the return, before introducing Pulitzer Prize–winning journalist David Cay Johnston, author of the *The Making of Donald Trump*, to discuss how he had discovered an envelope inside his mailbox, with no return address, containing a copy of Trump's 2005 two-page 1040 form.

While she was teasing out the reveal, the White House jumped ahead and released a copy of Trump's 2005 1040 to the media.

Maybe she shouldn't have sent that second tweet.

What was worse was that the numbers showed Trump actually paid $38 million in taxes that year.

Was that all? Where was the smoking gun?

The backlash—on Twitter and in the media—was instantaneous.

@MarkSimoneNY joked that her next episode would be on Donald Trumps 1997 dental records.

Even Anderson Cooper retweeted the obvious takeaway from @VanJones68:

If all we get tonight is that Trump paid $38M to America's government, that's a good night for Trump.

In any case, before the show had ended, *The Washington Post*, *The New York Times*, and numerous other publications had already posted stories of their own based on the White House release.

The next day, while the brickbats flew, Rachel defended her methods and deflected the criticism. "We broke the story correctly, were totally transparent about what we got, making it available in a way that made its importance understandable, and didn't either understate or overstate the meaning of this new piece of the Donald Trump financial puzzle. I'm really, really, really psyched that we broke this story.

"I really have no regrets at all. People were mad that it wasn't more scandalous. But that's not my fault, I did it right."

In any case, ratings that night hit a new record for the show when 4.1 million viewers tuned in, but Rachel's complex positions on controversial topics continued to alienate some viewers and critics, particularly when it came to her support for the National Rifle Association. "I have a lot of respect for what the NRA used to focus on and still in part focuses on, which is promoting marksmanship and shooting sports and conservation, and I think all of that stuff makes a lot of sense," she said.

"I'm not against the Second Amendment, but I am for rational gun control and I don't think it's incompatible to be a gun enthusiast, to enjoy shooting sports and hunting, and to also be in favor of gun control measures that make us a more safe and civil society," she said. "But I think that having a gun in my house makes it more likely that somebody will be shot in my house, so I don't think that a gun would make me safer."

The quickened news cycle caused by the Trump presidency was wreaking havoc on the staff of *TRMS*.

Pre-Trump, depending on the form of media, a typical news cycle lasted around twenty-four hours, allowing a story to go from leading off a TV or radio broadcast or appearing on the front page of a newspaper one day, before moving to later in the show or to an inside page—or dropping off the list entirely—within twenty-four hours or a few days.

But Trump changed the news cycle even before he took office by making outrageous claims, inciting reporters to dig up dirt on him to refute those claims, and repeating the process whenever he switched his story, sometimes within hours. Reporters were obligated to cover these changes, so it's natural that the turmoil of his presidency also shortened the news cycle. "This may be Trump's greatest trick, his tornado of news making has scrambled Americans' grasp of time and memory, producing a sort of sensory overload that can make even seismic events—of his creation or otherwise—disappear from the collective consciousness and public view," wrote *New York Times* journalist Matt Flegenheimer.

The whiplash-inducing news cycle also had a profound effect behind the scenes at the show, at least initially. "This administration is Chaos, Incorporated, and that means you can't plan ahead, ever," said Rachel.

"Trump has mastered the political media by causing you to lose focus and then re-center on whatever it is he's just said," she said.

"At some point, that can't be the story of every day. When somebody has proven to you that they are not telling the truth, that they lie regularly and don't feel bad about it even when they're caught, that is freeing because that means you are excused from ever having to listen to that person ever again in terms of trying to get factual information."

So after spending a few months reacting to the falsehoods coming out of the White House and from Trump's supporters in Washington, and eventually realizing that no one in the administration would be honest about what was *really* going on in the White House—aside from an occasional anonymous leak—Rachel added a second mission statement to the mix to account for the constantly shifting sands: "Don't pay attention to what they *say*, just focus on what they *do*," she said. "[Now] we basically cover them as if they are a silent movie."

This shift immediately brought the stress level down a notch or three. "I'm not going to talk about misstatements in the briefing room or the outrageous provocations from the president on social media, and I'm not going to play media wars where I get into fights with other people," she said. "Focusing is the thing I care the most about right now when I get on the air, but that's the hardest to do because it requires the most original thought."

She also decided to stop following the Twitter feeds coming out of the White House, which helped smooth over the rough edges of producing a nightly broadcast.

"The twenty-four-hour news cycle is really more like an eight-hour news cycle at this point because people are up at weird times, and they want to be able to get stuff as soon as it happens," she added, though some would say that it has since morphed into a four-hour cycle.

Rachel bemoaned the process, explaining her challenges on the air to viewers on April 25, 2018. "We finished the news meeting, planned the whole show, and I turned and looked at my producer and the staff and said, 'Doesn't it feel like a whole bunch of other stuff is about to break?'" Sure enough, it did. "Tonight we learned that [Rudy] Giuliani has just had his first meeting with special counsel Robert Mueller," she reported in the first minutes of the show.

But the warp-speed new normal of the news cycle was still a major stressor, requiring both Rachel and her staff to be more nimble even once the show went live since it was virtually a given that something in the news would change while Rachel was reporting on that very story to millions of viewers. So both Rachel and her staff learned to react on the fly most nights of the week, often modifying segments and even frantically calling around to convince a source to rush to the studio for a live appearance.

And whenever she discovered that a pro-Trump source had lied, he was cut from the list of potential guests for the show, and was no longer used for background research.

It worked. In May 2017, *The Rachel Maddow Show* was the most-viewed show on cable news, the first time she had topped Bill O'Reilly's show on Fox News and also CNN. Compared with a year earlier—even in the rush of the primary season— the show boosted its audience by 120 percent, while Fox News viewership dropped by 5 percent.

Even with the increased audience and revamped production of the show, Rachel realized it would be a twisty road ahead, and she counseled her staff to prepare for the long haul, though she could have also been advising her fans.

She then did what few TV hosts would do, much less pull off: She put her own spin on the topic by vaguely implicating her progressive and liberal audience as complicit, in the hopes of spurring them on to take action, however slight. Her "A-block" segment on the June 30, 2017, show served as a call to arms: "With a normal politician's normal political distraction . . . we're either distracted by it or we're not. [Trump's] strategy, though, it is really different. It's to sort of tap on the glass of your moral compass—'Is this thing on?' To try to make you feel implicated by your silence."

Around the same time, Rachel wrenched her back and had trouble walking around and sitting for a few days afterward. "I wrote to my mom about it and she said, 'Well, of course, you're not taking care of yourself.' I said, 'Oh, Mom. I don't think you can blame Trump for this,' but she said, 'Well, your life has been a little upturned.' My mom thinks I keep throwing my back out because of Jared [Kushner]. But you know, I don't know."

One of the ways in which she began to take care of herself was to take Fridays off during the summer. She maintained the same routine to keep herself sane and productive, reserving mornings off-limits when it came to work. "I'll go to the gym, or spend time with Susan, or sometimes, when the weather is nice, I'll go fishing before I go to work," she said. "I try to do something that is definitely not work."

For a while, she experimented with spreading out the work across a few more hours so that she didn't have to cram it into nine hours before airtime, but she found that counterproductive. "I've tried starting work at nine, but you can only have your brain lit up for that long before it starts to break down and you stop making sense and stop being creative," she said.

Despite her crazy schedule, she decided to pursue outside activities that she hadn't done before, including crafting a crossword puzzle for *The New York Times*, which appeared on March 2, 2018.

She was thrilled at her accomplishment. "I'm a childless, middle-aged, potbellied lesbian, and I don't have that much to be excited about in my life other than having a great job," she said. "This is kind of it, like there will never be a baby, but there's this freaking crossword puzzle, and I am very, very excited about it!"

She expanded her horizons at MSNBC as well, producing and

hosting *Bag Man*, a podcast series profiling Spiro Agnew, the vice president under Richard Nixon, and *Betrayal*, a documentary focusing on the 1968 presidential season and how Nixon conspired with the South Vietnamese government to win the election. In a way, she viewed both projects through the same lens as *Drift;* they were both topics that she felt deserved more airtime than she could provide on her show, and were particularly timely topics to cover, given present-day obstruction of the truth at the highest levels of government. But instead of devoting another book to one or both topics, she returned to one form she was familiar with, the documentary, and one that was unfamiliar, the podcast.

"When things are done in secret in our name, we can be held accountable for them, even if we can't hold accountable our government for directing it," she says. "And that feels very un-American to me."

She particularly enjoyed the process of uncovering the truth about Agnew, whose crimes and misdemeanors had been somewhat swept under the rug when juxtaposed with Nixon's, because she had believed that compared to the president's lies and sins in office, Agnew was more of a minor player. Once she started to dig into the research and uncovered the actual story, she was caught up in uncovering more of the drama, as well as revealing it to viewers. "If there's ever a job opening for a full-time storyteller about the life and legacy of Spiro T. Agnew, I might apply," she admitted.

And along with uncovering a little-known cornerstone in

American history, Rachel also enjoyed the process of learning how to tell a story in a completely new format, but she also admitted that burning the candle at both ends was taking a huge toll. "I am a husk of my former self," she said, adding that when she ticked everything off of her to-do list, she'd manage to take some time off and catch up on such much-needed sleep, though her co-workers knew she was just paying lip service to the idea.

On September 7, 2018, Rachel devoted the last segment of her show to celebrating its tenth anniversary the next day, where she sounded as if she didn't really believe that she had made it this far. "Tomorrow is the ten-year anniversary of this show, which means we're really freaking old," she said. "I mean, in cable news years, we're like one thousand. We're like Great-Uncle Pete who is always falling asleep in the Thanksgiving mashed potatoes."

She had further cause for celebration the following week when the show broke previous ratings yet again, with an average of more than 3.4 million nightly viewers for the week; the September 14 show garnered 3.66 million in the audience.

So what's next for Rachel?

Even though she's declared numerous times that she'd never run for political office, her fans continue to beg her to reconsider. "Anybody who knows me knows that I have no intention of running for office ever in my whole career," she said.

"I would be a terrible legislator. I don't want to ever raise money, I'm *afraid* of money," she admitted. "I can't even scratch a lottery ticket. The idea of asking people for money so that I could then be a politician makes me wanna shoot myself in the head. So, I don't ever, ever, ever wanna do it."

Besides, she still loved her job. "I have a really good job and I don't want to run for office. I don't want to serve in elected office, but I wish that more people who wanted me to, would, frankly," she said.

"No pundit should have anything to do with the practice of politics ever, ever, ever. It would be like taking the average caller into an ESPN show and letting him go, 'Snap the ball to Brady,' you just don't do it."

Even after completing the first decade of the show—something few shows can claim—Rachel did continue to ponder whether she was making the best use of her skills and philosophies. "I do worry if being a pundit is a worthwhile thing to be," she said.

At the same time, she also views the longevity of her show—and its format—as just as unlikely. "There's one very simple reason we persist," she said, "which is that there are some things you want to watch live . . . you still need a person who gets information and explains to you what's going on in a way you can visually connect with. That's what keeps me in business."

She also saw her role in light of the present political chaos as a necessary one. "I'm very, very proud to be part of the press corps in this country right now given the very, very good work that has happened thus far in terms of ferreting out the truth about this administration that they don't want known," she said.

Though she loves what she does, with a schedule that would break lesser mortals inside of a week, she has openly admitted the horrendous toll that it has taken on her free time and health. And as the 2020 presidential campaign heats up, it doesn't look as though she's going to get a chance to slack off anytime soon. "I anticipate we'll be working as hard, if not harder," said Cory Gnazzo.

Could she ever imagine leaving the show, perhaps cutting back to a more reasonable schedule and doing a couple of documentaries and podcasts a year and hitting the lecture circuit?

As she admits, it's highly unlikely. "I have the best job on earth. I get paid to talk on TV about what I want to without editorial interference from anybody five nights a week, fifty weeks a year," she said.

"I think helping people understand what is going on in the world and what is going on in your country is a noble thing to do," she said. "[And] I think I have found something I am good at."

ACKNOWLEDGMENTS

As usual, eternal thanks go to Superagent, a.k.a Scott Mendel, as well as to everyone at St. Martin's Press, including Tom Dunne, Stephen Power, Lisa Bonvissuto, John Karle, and Sara Beth Haring.

NOTES

Introduction

2   "and I don't hold back": Dyana Bagby, "Two 'L-words,'" *Southern Voice*, January 28, 2005.

2   "I've stolen some more deserving person's television show": *Late Show with David Letterman*, April 4, 2013.

2   "I've never seen anyone prepare like she does": *American Prospect*, October 1, 2008.

3   "I am not a model of mental health": Interview, New York Film Academy, May 4, 2015.

3   "I want to convince myself that my existence matters": Julia Baird, "Rachel Maddow Comes Out on Top," *Newsweek*, November 21, 2008.

3   "She wanted to change the world": Jessica Pressler, "The Dr. Maddow Show," *New York*, November 2, 2008.

3   "despite being a liberal": Marisa Guthrie, "Rachel Maddow: How This Wonky-Tonk Woman Won TV," *Hollywood Reporter*, October 5, 2011.

3   "regardless of who has them": Robert Sullivan, "Shaping the News," *Vogue*, January 2009.

4   "no one is angry, no one is bloody": Marisa Guthrie, "Rachel Maddow: How This Wonky-Tonk Woman Won TV," *Hollywood Reporter*, October 5, 2011.

4   "She's a person of principle": Marisa Guthrie, "Rachel Maddow: How this Honky-Tonk Woman Won TV," *The Hollywood Reporter*, October 5, 2011.

4   "the Fourth Amendment is personally wired into my DNA": Interview with Rachel Maddow, *The Torch*, ACLU, Fall 2007.

4   "taking care of the tumor and fixing it": Ben Wallace-Wells, "Rachel Maddow's Quiet War," *Rolling Stone*, June 27, 2012.

5   "in a much better way": Jessica Pressler, "The Dr. Maddow Show," *New York*, November 2, 2008.

5   "I think is meant to humiliate people": Ibid.

5   "to not like her": Ibid.

5   "And we are at sea": Ken Tucker, "Rooting for Lefty," *New York*, July 18, 2005.

5   "you might as well try to win": Matea Gold, "MSNBC's New Liberal Spark Plug," *Los Angeles Times*, September 29, 2008.

Chapter 1: *"Who Is That Kid and Where Did She Come From?"*

7   "wanting to check everything out": Erin Bried, *How to Rock Your Baby* (New York: Hyperion, 2012), xvi.

7   "and where did she come from?": Robert Rouza, "CVHS Grad to Host Nationwide MSNBC Show," *Castro Valley Forum*, August 27, 2008.

8   "or do something really different": Erin Bried *How to Rock Your Baby*, xxiv.

9   "and people that were overlooked": Joe Garofoli, "Activist Aims to Break Rules of Cable News," *San Francisco Chronicle*, September 11, 2008.

9   "they couldn't afford to staff it anymore": ACWA Fall Conference, Long Beach, California, December 3, 2008.

9   "that water is power": Ibid.

9   "'what went wrong in your day?'": Erin Bried *How to Rock Your Baby*, xxv.

9   "going to take care of it?": Ibid.

10   "and then went straight back home": *The Ezra Klein Show*, February 9, 2016.

10   "When I see those, I get misty": Robert Nesti, "Reality Check with Rachel Maddow," *The Edge*, July 27, 2006.

10   know you can't see the picture": Robert Sullivan, "Shaping the News," *Vogue*, January 2009.

11   "All I remember is the feeling of dislike": Julia Baird, "Rachel Maddow Comes Out on Top," *Newsweek*, November 21, 2008.

11   "very conservative, nasty little town": Hadley Freeman, "Rachel Maddow: 'I'm Definitely Not an Autocutie,'" *The Guardian*, April 25, 2011.

11   "'Okay, we're not going to discuss it anymore'": Chuck Barney, "Maddow Newest Talk-Show Titan," *Contra Costa Times*, October 18, 2008.

12   "the people would glow a different color": *The Ezra Klein Show*, February 9, 2016.

12   "please go and beat them up": Ibid.

12   "it was probably the apex of my coolness": "I Am Rachel Maddow: Ask Me Anything!," Reddit, March 11, 2013.

12   "I was best at being the conductor": "Rachel Maddow: 25 Things You Don't Know About Me ('I'm a Terrible Correspondent')," *Us Weekly*, July 17, 2016.

13   "didn't reflect that aspect of my personality": Catie Lazarus, "Rachel Maddow," *Employee of the Month*, January 16, 2013.

13   "take such an outsider's perspective seemed so great": Hadley Freeman, "Rachel Maddow: 'I'm Definitely Not an Autocutie,'" *The Guardian*, April 25, 2011.

14   "and this may be all you get": Louise France, "I'm Not a TV Anchor Babe. I'm a Big Lesbian Who Looks Like a Man," *The Guardian*, February 7, 2009.

14   "I wanted that to be *my* car": *The Howard Stern Show*, May 24, 2017.

14   "in my life than to the men": David Hochman, "*Playboy* Interview: Rachel Maddow Talks Hillary, Hate Mail & More in Our First Non-Nude Issue," *Playboy*, February 2016.

14   "So *that's* what's going on below my chin": Alix Olson, "Rachel Maddow: Straight Talk," *Velvet Park*, Summer 2005.

15   "'they play softball and I will never'": "The *Out* 100: The Men & Women Who Made 2008," *Out*, November 2, 2008.

15   "hard for them to accept me": *The Howard Stern Show*, May 24, 2017.

15   "about those issues at that time": Joe Garofoli, "Activist Aims to Break Rules of Cable News," *San Francisco Chronicle*, September 11, 2008.

15   "it was not going to be very safe": *The Howard Stern Show*, May 24, 2017.

15   "I never thought I'd reach drinking age": Louise France, "I'm Not a TV Anchor Babe. I'm a Big Lesbian Who Looks Like a Man," *The Guardian*, February 7, 2009.

15   "I was going to have a hard life": *The Howard Stern Show*, May 24, 2017.

16   "place I wanted to be a gay person in": Janet Malcolm, "Rachel Maddow: Trump's TV Nemesis," *New Yorker*, October 9, 2017.

16   "that's the thing that I should do": Catie Lazarus, "Rachel Maddow," *Employee of the Month*, January 16, 2013.

17   The car's broken: Rachel Maddow at the Steinbeck Center, February 25, 2012.

17   "this better be building toward something": *The Howard Stern Show*, May 24, 2017.

17   "It was a blessing in disguise": Louise France, "I'm Not a TV Anchor Babe. I'm a Big Lesbian Who Looks Like a Man," *The Guardian*, February 7, 2009.

18   "went into her academics": Robert B. Maddow, "Water Supply, Water Rights and Other Legal Issues at the East Bay Municipal Utility District, 1972–1993," Bancroft Library, University of California, Berkeley, 2003.

19   "I've truly wanted to say for the past four years": High school graduation speech, June 1990.

19   "give something back to this town": Ibid.

19   "because tonight we become those elders": Ibid.

19   "I could actually do anything at that point": Rachel Maddow at the Steinbeck Center, February 25, 2012.

Chapter 2: *Breaking Free and Coming Out*

21   "did not know how to do college": *The Ezra Klein Show*, February 9, 2016.

22   "I had no idea how any of this worked": Ibid.

22   "social change through non-violent action": Columbae House Description, Stanford Residential Education website.

23   "stolen some more deserving person's spot": *Late Show with David Letterman*, April 3, 2013.

23   "I maybe had leadership potential": Catie Lazarus, "Rachel Maddow," *Employee of the Month*, January 16, 2013.

23   "in-line skating and jogging and email": Alix Olson, "Rachel Maddow: Straight Talk," *Velvet Park*, Summer 2005.

23   "I saw among college freshmen": Terry Gross, "Rachel Maddow: The *Fresh Air* Interview," NPR, March 27, 2012.

23   If she can be out, I can be out: Shauna Swartz, "Radio Star Rachel Maddow," AfterEllen.com, January 29, 2007.

24   "they still wanted to say them": Robin Mathison, "Freshman Lesbians Face Coming Out with Fear, Relief," *Stanford Daily*, March 4, 1991.

24   "I was waiting for somebody to ask me": Ibid.

24   "to provoke people who couldn't handle it": Alix Olson, "Rachel Maddow: Straight Talk," *Velvet Park*, Summer 2005.

24   "there was a posse of people behind me": Robin Mathison, "Freshman Lesbians Face Coming Out with Fear, Relief," *Stanford Daily*, March 4, 1991.

24   "my seventeen-year-old mind thought that it would": Shauna Swartz, "Radio Star Rachel Maddow," AfterEllen.com, January 29, 2007.

24   "I was ninety percent attitude": Julia Baird, "Rachel Maddow Comes Out on Top," *Newsweek*, November 21, 2008.

25   "to throw something up in people's faces": Terry Gross, "Rachel Maddow: The *Fresh Air* Interview," NPR, March 27, 2012.

25   "'I'm going to have courage'": Ben Wallace-Wells, "Rachel Maddow's Quiet War," *Rolling Stone*, June 27, 2012.

25   "the many girls I was sleeping with": Hadley Freeman, "Rachel Maddow: 'I'm Definitely Not an Autocutie,'" *The Guardian*, April 25, 2011.

26   "I don't blame them. I was obnoxious": *The Howard Stern Show*, May 24, 2017.

26   "We just wanted her to be safe": Julia Baird, "Rachel Maddow Comes Out on Top," *Newsweek*, November 21, 2008.

27   "in prevention and awareness": Bob Ickes, "Maddow About You," *POZ*, June 1, 2009.

27   "roll a rubber tire on your schlonger?": Joel Stein, "Japanese Condoms Score Big in Fifth Annual Rubber Match," *Stanford Daily*, May 17, 1991.

29   "I had no idea what to do": Beth Berselli, "Nowhere to Go: Harassment of Gays Frequent, Rarely Reported," *Stanford Daily*, March 28, 1994.

29   "studying and doing in school": "Stanford University News Service, "Two Alumnae Win Rhodes, Marshall Scholarships," Stanford University, December 13, 1994.

29   "so it goes unchecked": Robin Mathison, "Freshman Lesbians Face Coming Out with Fear, Relief," *Stanford Daily*, March 4, 1991.

30   "I might not have done otherwise": Stanford University News Service, "Two Alumnae Win Rhodes, Marshall Scholarships," Stanford University, December 13, 1994.

30   "I didn't feel very welcome at Stanford": Colleen M. Lee, "The Inside Story from Rachel Maddow," *Curve*, October 9, 2008.

31   "culturally to be part of": Aaron Sekhri, "Rachel Maddow Visits Stanford for First Time Since Graduating," *Stanford Daily*, March 16, 2013.

31   "I felt culturally alienated": Joe Garofoli, "Activist Aims to Break Rules of Cable News," *San Francisco Chronicle*, September 11, 2008.

31   "What do I wanna be when I grow up?": Interview, New York Film Academy, May 4, 2015.

31   "boring freaking legal policy you could possibly study": Ibid.

32   "treat people very badly": Bob Ickes, "Maddow About You," *POZ*, June 2009.

32   "come around every few years or so": "Two Alumnae Win Rhodes,

Marshall Scholarships," Stanford University News Service, December 13, 1994.

32 "and dedication to public service, bar none": Ibid.

32 "my faith in the next generation": Ibid.

32 "to that thesis as a model": Jessica Pressler, "The Dr. Maddow Show," *New York*, November 2, 2008.

33 "to take care of myself as much as possible": *The Ezra Klein Show*, February 9, 2016.

33 "could count as evidence and what couldn't": Barrett Sheridan, "Making Airwaves," *Stanford Magazine*, May/June 2008.

34 "and I didn't do that at all": Colleen M. Lee, "The Inside Story from Rachel Maddow," *Curve*, October 2008.

35 "I felt my country was declaring war on me": Howard Kurtz, "Rachel Maddow, MSNBC's Newest Left Hand," *Washington Post*, August 27, 2008.

Chapter 3: *Activism and Oxford*

37 "in California, and in the country": Rachel Maddow, "Courage!," *Huffington Post*, September 13, 2006.

38 "and generzally worked my tail off": "Profile of Success: Rachel Maddow," Stanford University Career Development Center, December 5, 2004.

38 "chained myself to someone's desk": Rachel Maddow, "Courage!," *Huffington Post*, September 13, 2006.

38 "to be able to participate": Bob Ickes, "Maddow About You," *POZ*, June 2009.

39 "I was a very, very slow barista": Michele Greppi, "The Insider: Rachel Maddow Ready for Debut," *TV Week*, September 2008.

39 "Our most popular drink was the five-shot espresso": *Washington Journal*, C-SPAN, August 21, 2007.

40 "and make them want to be part of you": Catie Lazarus, "Rachel Maddow," *Employee of the Month*, January 16, 2013.

40 "I worked on stuff that I could get done": Q&A Session, McCoy

Family Center for Ethics in Society at Stanford University, March 16, 2013.

40   "not everybody approaches these things this way": Ibid.

40   "I'm just not wired that way": Catie Lazarus, "Rachel Maddow," *Employee of the Month*, January 16, 2013.

41   "very impressive people going for this": Kevin Fagan, "2 Bay Women Are Rhodes Scholars," *San Francisco Chronicle*, December 12, 1994.

41   "one of her roommates was trying to get a Marshall at the time": Robert B. Maddow, "Water Supply, Water Rights and Other Legal Issues at the East Bay Municipal Utility District, 1972–1993," Bancroft Library, University of California, Berkeley, 2003.

42   "I did it again to get it blue": "Two Alumnae Win Rhodes, Marshall Scholarships," Stanford University News Service, December 13, 1994.

42   "and branching out into other social justice issues": Colleen Kruger, "Two Alums Win Prestigious Awards," *Stanford Daily*, January 9, 1995.

42   "it's not what I'm about": Ibid.

42   "to get a graduate degree for free": *The Ezra Klein Show*, February 9, 2016.

43   "I spent three days as a master's candidate": Ibid.

44   "the life of Rhodes gatherings with her dry wit": Banuta Rubess, "So Weird and So Awesome: Rachel Maddow California Rhodes Scholar, 1995," RhodesProject.com/scholar-contributions.

44   "is, sadly, a notable thing": Ken Tucker, "Rooting for Lefty," *New York*, July 18, 2005.

45   "wouldn't have even known that neighborhood existed": Jessica Pressler, "The Dr. Maddow Show," *New York*, November 2, 2008.

46   "I managed to sustain it": Hadley Freeman, "Rachel Maddow: 'I'm Definitely Not an Autocutie,'" *The Guardian*, April 25, 2011.

46   "pushing for progressive victories": "Rachel Maddow, Another Progressive Radio Host Well Worth Listening To," BuzzFlash, September 18, 2007.

46   "want to blow my head off": Edward Levine, "A Pundit in the Country," *New York Times*, October 17, 2008.

47   "only shame and panic that make me write a paragraph": Margaret Heilbrun, "Q&A: Rachel Maddow, Author of *Drift*," *Library Journal*, March 20, 2012.

47   "that I would never get it done": *The Ezra Klein Show*, February 9, 2016.

47   "it could work": Ibid.

47   "sounded like the seventeenth circle of hell": *The Howard Stern Show*, May 24, 2017.

48   "it *was* the seventeenth circle of hell": Ibid.

48   "That sounds pretty miserable too!": *The Ezra Klein Show*, February 9, 2016.

48   "we had to sleep in hats": Alix Olson, "Rachel Maddow: Straight Talk," *Velvet Park*, Summer 2005.

Chapter 4: *Love and Radio*

49   "failure is a real possibility": *The Ezra Klein Show*, February 9, 2016.

49   "the world and my place in it": Dyana Bagby, "Two 'L-words,'" *Southern Voice*, January 28, 2005.

50   "we planned to release [the news]": Zach Carter, "How Rachel Maddow Helped Force Bill Clinton's Support for Mandela's AIDS Plan," *Huffington Post*, December 6, 2013.

50   "'You have to go to New Hampshire in the morning!'": Ibid.

51   "I was bad at everything": *The Howard Stern Show*, May 24, 2017.

51   "I was great at it": Craig Smith, "Rise of a 'Bucket Washer,'" *Pittsburgh Tribune-Review*, March 21, 2009.

51   "suspicious of recycling for my whole life": "My Worst Summer Job: Rachel Maddow," *The Tonight Show Starring Jimmy Fallon*, August 21, 2015.

53   "It was crazy": *The Howard Stern Show*, May 24, 2017.

53   "bluebirds and comets and stars": Janet Malcolm, "Rachel Maddow: Trump's TV Nemesis," *New Yorker*, October 9, 2017.

53   "Okay, my whole life is different now": Julia Baird, "Rachel Maddow Comes Out on Top," *Newsweek*, November 21, 2008.

53   "You're hired": *The Howard Stern Show*, May 24, 2017.

53   "So hot. *So* hot": Jessica Pressler, "The Dr. Maddow Show," *New York*, November 2, 2008.

53   "two more days and that was it": *The Howard Stern Show*, May 24, 2017.

54   "big part of who we are": Loren King, "Pinhole Orientation," *The Princetown Banner*, October 22, 2009.

54   "I had never wanted to": Louise France, "I'm Not a TV Anchor Babe. I'm a Big Lesbian Who Looks Like a Man," *The Guardian*, February 7, 2009.

54   "I was really good with the AR-15": Terry Gross "Rachel Maddow: The *Fresh Air* Interview," NPR, March 27, 2012.

55   "for having brought in some newbie liberals": Ibid.

56   "and did an on-air audition": Rachel Maddow at the Steinbeck Center, February 25, 2012.

56   "Who is this fourteen-year-old boy pulling up in a pickup truck?": Mark Leibovich, "Rachel Maddow," *New York Times*, June 7, 2013.

56   "He said, 'You're hired'": Terry Gross "Rachel Maddow: The *Fresh Air* Interview," NPR, March 27, 2012.

56   "I'd figured this out before I was twenty-six": Rory O'Connor, "Rachel Maddow: Progressive Media's Next Mainstream Star," Maddow Fans.com, April 9, 2008.

57   "'cause every third Sunday there's brunch": Catie Lazarus, "Rachel Maddow," *Employee of the Month*, January 16, 2013.

57   "I can smell my eyeballs burning": "Rachel Maddow: 25 Things You Don't Know About Me ('I'm a Terrible Correspondent')," *Us Weekly*, July 17, 2016.

57   "better than it had been with my glasses": Balin Eye & Laser Center website.

58   "and that offended some people": Interview: Rachel Maddow Talks Hillary, Hate Mail & More in Our First Non-Nude Issue," *Playboy*, February 2016.

58   "It sounds mean, but she loved it": Mark Leibovich, "Rachel Maddow," *New York Times*, June 7, 2013.

58   "the funniest thing he'd ever done in his life": "Lesley Stahl Asks Rachel Maddow: What Do You Do @ 7 on Sunday?," Women on the Web, January 26, 2009.

58   "What is she doing here?": Jessica Pressler, "The Dr. Maddow Show," *New York*, November 2, 2008.

59   "I thought I would be an [activist] forever": Terry Gross, "Rachel Maddow: The *Fresh Air* Interview," NPR, March 27, 2012.

59   "in order to shorten your sentence": Interview, New York Film Academy, May 4, 2015.

60   "It's a very instrumental thing," Catie Lazarus, "Rachel Maddow," *Employee of the Month*, January 16, 2013.

61   "Who makes the decisions?": *The Ezra Klein Show*, February 9, 2016.

61   "All right, now we've got a hearing": Ibid.

62   "to do what we wanted": Ibid.

62   "Other than the hours, it was pure joy": "Rachel Maddow: The *Fresh Air* Interview," NPR, March 27, 2012.

62   "Rachel could make toast and salsa": Michelle Tan, "MSNBC's Rachel Maddow at Home & Unplugged," *People*, April 12, 2010.

62   "it's not what you hear on the radio most of the time": "Susan Mikula: Art, Inspiration and Heart," GoGetYourGirlOn.com, February 19, 2010.

Chapter 5: *Switching Gears*

66   "I just wanted to be back in there": Catie Lazarus, "Rachel Maddow," *Employee of the Month*, January 16, 2013.

66   "and I wanted to be helpful": Interview, New York Film Academy, May 4, 2015.

66   "I missed the opportunity to explain stuff": Ted Johnson, "Maddow's Unique Style Spikes Ratings," *Variety*, March 6, 2009.

68   "and I'd play this big quacking sound effect": Michele Greppi, "The Insider: Rachel Maddow Ready for Debut," *TV Week*, September 2008.

68   "and get the concert tickets from me": Ibid.

68   "and have something to say": Catie Lazarus, "Rachel Maddow," *Employee of the Month*, January 16, 2013.

69   "because you can't be too self-conscious": Michele Greppi, "The Insider: Rachel Maddow Ready for Debut," *TV Week*, September 2008.

69 "what I needed to be putting my brain into": *The Ezra Klein Show*, February 9, 2016.

70 "between yourself and that trigger": Bob Ickes, "Maddow About You," *POZ*, June 2009.

71 "like a very big leap": Catie Lazarus, "Rachel Maddow," *Employee of the Month*, January 16, 2013.

71 "They had no business hiring me": Rebecca Traister, "Rachel Maddow's Life and Career," *The Nation*, August 18, 2008.

72 "I realized if I worked hard I might get better at it": Rachel Maddow at the Steinbeck Center, February 25, 2012.

72 "So I pulled out all the stops": Interview, New York Film Academy, May 4, 2015.

72 "and wouldn't take no for an answer": Julie A. Weisberg, "Rachel Maddow: Out on Air America, Shaking Up the Airwaves," *Page One Q*, June 19, 2007.

72 "bring him tapes of my hosted music show": Rory O'Connor, "Rachel Maddow: Progressive Media's Next Mainstream Star," MaddowFans .com, April 9, 2008.

72 "this sort of joy": Ben Wallace-Wells, "Rachel Maddow's Quiet War," *Rolling Stone*, June 27, 2012.

73 "and the next day, I wasn't": Bob Ickes, "Maddow About You," *POZ*, June 2009.

74 "in order to understand it better": Catie Lazarus, "Rachel Maddow," *Employee of the Month*, January 16, 2013.

74 "We essentially treat [the apartment] like a hotel room": Jen Chung, "Rachel Maddow, Host of 'The Rachel Maddow Show,'" Gothamist .com, April 24, 2009.

Chapter 6: *Air America*

76 "Liberals are ready to fight": Russell Shorto, "Al Franken, Seriously So," *New York Times Sunday Magazine*, March 21, 2004.

77 "it seemed much bigger than me": Catie Lazarus, "Rachel Maddow," *Employee of the Month*, January 16, 2013.

77 "we're competing for ratings": Dyana Bagby, "Two 'L-words,'" *Southern Voice*, January 28, 2005.

77 "there is high emotion on the liberal side": Russell Shorto, "Al Franken, Seriously So," *New York Times Sunday Magazine*, March 21, 2004.

77 "take off and be this big deal": Catie Lazarus, "Rachel Maddow," *Employee of the Month*, January 16, 2013.

78 "telling what's going on in the news": *The Ezra Klein Show*, February 9, 2016.

78 "Why don't you do it?": Ibid.

79 "I'm the straight man of the three": Andrew Varnon, "The Return of Rachel Maddow," *Valley Advocate*, June 24, 2004.

79 "brings it back to the facts": Etelka Lehoczky, "Left and Centered," *The Advocate*, August 31, 2004.

79 "represent that voice that's not heard": Ibid.

79 "we can appreciate the other's type": Bosie Crawford, "Last Call," *Metrosource*, 2005.

80 "there was something special about her": Sean Braswell, "Air America + The Rise of Rachel Maddow," Ozy.com, March 31, 2014.

80 "there's no turning back": Dyana Bagby, "Two 'L-words': Morning Host Adds 'Lesbian' to 'Liberal Radio's Success,'" *Southern Voice Atlanta*, January 28, 2005.

81 "radio is a medium": Deborah Caulfield Rybak, "A Bumpy Takeoff for Air America Liberal Radio Network," *Star Tribune*, May 15, 2004.

82 "there is a market for different political views": Dyana Bagby, "Two 'L-words,'" *Southern Voice*, January 28, 2005.

83 "'I can bring you the beer and pretzel folks'": Rick Bird, "Jerry's Show Goes National," *Cincinnati Post*, March 24, 2005.

84 "you're wasting a lot of people's time": Neal Justin, "She Zags, She Zigs, but She Can't Dance," *Star Tribune*, September 17, 2008.

85 "and my interest in fart jokes": Jane Burns, "Radio Host Finds Right Mix for Political Talk," *Capital Times*, October 16, 2007.

85 "of the mission of this overall show": Andrew Varnon, "Poking the White Underbelly," *Valley Advocate*, May 19, 2005.

Chapter 7: *Taking Off*

87   "but it sure was good for Air America": Julia Angwin and Sarah Mc-Bride, "Radio's Bush-Bashing Air America Is Back in Fighting Form," *Wall Street Journal*, January 20, 2005.

88   "and they can fight to the end of the show," Interview, New York Film Academy, May 4, 2015.

88   "if there ever was one": Matea Gold, "MSNBC's New Liberal Spark Plug," *Los Angeles Times*, September 29, 2008.

88   You were in prison when I was born: Andrew Varnon, "Poking the White Underbelly," *Valley Advocate*, May 19, 2005.

88   "I thought it was hilarious": Interview, New York Film Academy, May 4, 2015.

89   "and he's not condescending": Clara Jeffery, "Rachel Maddow's Star Power," *Mother Jones*, January/February 2009.

89   "even when his views are totally toxic": David Bauder, "Odd Couple: Rachel Maddow and Pat Buchanan," Associated Press, October 5, 2008.

89   "And that's how he became Uncle Pat": Interview, New York Film Academy, May 4, 2015.

90   "that makes me a raving liberal": Interview with Rachel Maddow, *The Torch*, ACLU, Fall 2007.

90   "that doesn't make room for people like me": Transcript, "The Scholar & Feminist XIX: Women as Changemakers: Building and Using Political Power," Barnard College, 2005.

90   "'now how does this relate to gay marriage?'": Alix Olson, "Rachel Maddow: Straight Talk," *Velvet Park*, Summer 2005.

91   "it does force you to get right to your point": David Hinckley, "Maddow Likes Idea Radio Has Influence," *New York Daily News*, November 6, 2006.

91   "so you have to be a thing": *The Ezra Klein Show*, February 9, 2016.

91   "things should be revealed on the show": Ibid.

91   "I'm not that pretty": Howard Kurtz, "Rachel Maddow, MSNBC's Newest Left Hand," *Washington Post*, August 27, 2008.

91   "'I look this way on purpose!'": Alix Olson, "Rachel Maddow: Straight Talk," *Velvet Park*, Summer 2005.

92   "but more than that, she's fast—really fast": Howard Kurtz, "Rachel Maddow Seizes Her Moment at Post–Keith Olbermann MSNBC," *Daily Beast*, February 27, 2011.

92   "people who disagree with her": Howard Kurtz, "Rachel Maddow, MSNBC's Newest Left Hand," *Washington Post*, August 27, 2008.

92   "or lose her indulgent affection, either": Jeff Simon, "Air America Foundering in Turbulence," *Buffalo News*, October 24, 2006.

93   "since Abbie Hoffman circa *The Dick Cavett Show*": Ken Tucker, "Rooting for Lefty," *New York*, July 18, 2005.

93   "I'll just meld with my couch": Joe Garofoli, "Activist Aims to Break Rules of Cable News," *San Francisco Chronicle*, September 11, 2008.

93   "how you're *supposed* to be political on television": Ken Tucker, "Rooting for Lefty," *New York*, July 18, 2005.

94   "more than half the fun": Ben Wallace-Wells, "Rachel Maddow's Quiet War," *Rolling Stone*, June 27, 2012.

94   "You wouldn't put *The Sopranos* on Comedy Central": Jessica Pressler, "The Dr. Maddow Show," *New York*, November 2, 2008.

94   "I am unattractive when I scream": Interview with Rachel Maddow, *The Torch*, ACLU, Fall 2007.

95   "I get to yell at him in person": Sasha Issenberg, "A Liberal Pundit Soars to a Prominent Perch," *Boston Globe*, September 8, 2008.

95   "Tucker deserves a lot of credit for that": Colleen M. Lee, "The Inside Story from Rachel Maddow": *Curve*, October 9, 2008.

95   "the stuff they say in public": "Fresh Air," *Out*, May 2006.

96   "I'm sure I'm for either, though": William Henderson, "Caught in the Political Crossfire," *The Advocate*, June 16, 2006.

96   "That was unsettling": Ibid.

96   "as long as I can remember": Terry Gross, "Rachel Maddow: The *Fresh Air* Interview," NPR, March 27, 2012.

97   "oh, hey, this is exciting": "Rachel Maddow, Another Progressive Radio Host Well Worth Listening To," BuzzFlash, September 18, 2007.

97 "I just sort of disappear": Terry Gross, "Rachel Maddow: The *Fresh Air* Interview," NPR, March 27, 2012.

97 "until it slows down enough so I can get off": Ibid.

98 "and go back to my life as an activist": Julie A. Weisberg, "Rachel Maddow: Out on Air America, Shaking Up the Airwaves," *Page One Q*, June 19, 2007.

98 "or at the end of your season, 'Did you win?'": Bob Ickes, "Maddow About You," *POZ*, June 2009.

98 "we do five hours for two hours, which is obscene": Robert Nesti, "Reality Check with Rachel Maddow," *The Edge*, July 27, 2006.

98 "really highly produced show": Julie A. Weisberg, "Rachel Maddow: Out on Air America, Shaking Up the Airwaves," *Page One Q*, June 19, 2007.

98 "It's a very strange, alienating lifestyle": Robert Nesti, "Reality Check with Rachel Maddow," *The Edge*, July 27, 2006.

99 "It's your day, but it's my night": Susan Brenna, "They Look Nothing Like Rush Limbaugh," *New York Times*, November 13, 2005.

99 "we have this beautiful house to come back to": Eric Goldscheider, "Weekday Bantering Is Balanced by Quiet N.E. Weekends," *Boston Globe*, February 24, 2005.

99 "Thanks for listening!": Alix Olson, "Rachel Maddow: Straight Talk," *Velvet Park*, Summer 2005.

100 "and here was this butch dyke!": Ibid.

100 "which is hurting my I-look-like-a-seventeen-year-old-boy experience!": Bosie Crawford, "Last Call," *Metrosource*, 2005.

Chapter 8: *Punditry*

102 "'but on this story, she'll be perfect!'": Michele Greppi, "The Insider: Rachel Maddow Ready for Debut," *TV Week*, September 2008.

102 "It was spectacular": "Rachel Maddow, Another Progressive Radio Host Well Worth Listening To," BuzzFlash, September 18, 2007.

103 "if you're laughing and entertained": Robert Nesti, "Reality Check with Rachel Maddow," *The Edge*, July 27, 2006.

103 "So I try to do both": Steve Krakauer, "So What Do You Do, MSNBC Host Rachel Maddow?," mediabistro, May 6, 2009.

104 "and I'm happy to have had it": Robert Nesti, "Reality Check with Rachel Maddow," *The Edge*, July 27, 2006.

104 "especially when you're an out, commie dyke": Colleen M. Lee, "The Inside Story from Rachel Maddow," *Curve*, October 9, 2008.

104 "as a political operation": Interview, New York Film Academy, May 4, 2015.

105 "We're trying to meet a need that does not exist": Catie Lazarus, "Rachel Maddow," *Employee of the Month*, January 16, 2013.

106 "I'm not going to stop dating": Howard Kurtz, "Rachel Maddow, MSNBC's Newest Left Hand," *Washington Post*, August 26, 2008.

106 "just so cheerful and hopeful and likable": Susan Brenna, "They Look Nothing Like Rush Limbaugh," *New York Times*, November 13, 2005.

106 "using one live on national television": Aaron Barnhart, "MSNBC's Chuck Todd and Rachel Maddow Are Young, Geeky and Hot," *Kansas City Star*, June 14, 2008.

107 "gay people bring to everything we do": Shauna Swartz, "Radio Star Rachel Maddow," AfterEllen.com, January 29, 2007.

107 "because of what I look like": Julie A. Weisberg, "Rachel Maddow: Out on Air America, Shaking Up the Airwaves," *Page One Q*, June 19, 2007.

107 "it created a sort of affirmative action impulse for pundits": Kay Steiger, "Five Minutes With: Rachel Maddow," Campus Progress.org, June 20, 2008.

108 "it's probably better for me not to take sides": Rebecca Traister, "Rachel Maddow's Life and Career," *The Nation*, July 30, 2008.

108 "it is just a shade shy of dim": F. Brinley Bruton, "Voice of America's Left," *New Statesman*, April 17, 2006.

109 "Look at me, I look like a dude": Rebecca Traister, "Rachel Maddow's Life and Career," *The Nation*, July 30, 2008.

109 "really, really hard": Jessica Pressler, "The Dr. Maddow Show," *New York*, November 2, 2008.

109 "it makes me feel like my life has meaning": Ibid.

109 "which causes me to do extra reading and preparation": Suzan Colon, "The New American Classic," *The Advocate*, December 2, 2008.

110 "on Air America for a long time": Rebecca Traister, "Rachel Maddow's Life and Career," *The Nation*, July 30, 2008.

110 "what they want to do about me": Jacques Steinberg, "Now in Living Rooms, the Host Apparent," *New York Times*, July 17, 2008.

110 "she's at the top": Ibid.

110 "If O'Reilly, Hannity, and Beck can [host both], so can I": Rebecca Traister, "Rachel Maddow's Life and Career," *The Nation*, July 30, 2008.

110 "I'm saying yes every time they ask me to be on television": Jacques Steinberg, "Now in Living Rooms, the Host Apparent," *New York Times*, July 17, 2008.

111 "Keith isn't the best way to go": Rebecca Traister, "Rachel Maddow's Life and Career," *The Nation*, July 30, 2008.

Chapter 9: *A Show of Her Own*

113 "Rachel would get an audience after Keith": Scott Pierce, "MSNBC's Maddow Thrives," *Deseret News*, February 26, 2009.

113–14 "one of the signature brands of the entire company": Brian Stelter, "MSNBC Takes Incendiary Hosts from Anchor Seat," *New York Times*, September 7, 2008.

114 "the final leg of the political race this year": Bill Carter, "MSNBC Changes Prime-Time Lineup," *New York Times*, August 19, 2008.

114 "four-night infomercial": Felix Gillette, "It's a Maddow, Maddow World," *New York*, August 28, 2008.

115 "it is actually the right call": Bill Carter, "MSNBC Changes Prime Time Lineup," *New York Times*, August 19, 2008.

115 "I want to remain a veal chop": Sasha Issenberg, "A Liberal Pundit Soars to a Prominent Perch," *Boston Globe*, September 8, 2008.

116 "Or more quiet": Ben Wallace-Wells, "Rachel Maddow's Quiet War," *Rolling Stone*, June 27, 2012.

116 "we can make sense of this world together": Robert Sullivan, "Shaping the News," *Vogue*, January 2009.

117 "so I have the best lead-in in cable news": Clara Jeffery, "Rachel Maddow's Star Power," *Mother Jones*, January/February 2009.

117 "being the first *blank* is always important": Howard Kurtz, "Rachel Maddow, MSNBC's Newest Left Hand," *Washington Post*, August 27, 2008.

117 "they call you an overnight sensation and claim your success": "The *Out* 100: The Men & Women Who Made 2008," *Out*, November 2, 2008.

118 "and assume people can come along with you": Morning News at 9, KTLA, Los Angeles, July 30, 2009.

118 "Americans absorb information in a lot of different ways": Alissa Quart, "The Sarcastic Times," *Columbia Journalism Review*, March/April 2009.

118 "people want someone collating or commenting on information": Ibid.

118 "My whole thing is to let Rachel be Rachel": Robert Sullivan, "Shaping the News," *Vogue*, January 2009.

119 "it's my fault, not the corporate network's fault": Rachel Maddow at the Steinbeck Center, February 25, 2012.

119 "and catfights among the channel's aging, white male divas": Alessandra Stanley, "A Fresh Female Face Amid Cable Schoolboys," *New York Times*, September 24, 2008.

119 "to attempt bludgeoning anyone with them": Troy Patterson, "Smart Woman," Slate.com, September 9, 2008.

119 "to major politico pundit in such a short order": Banuta Rubess, "So Weird and So Awesome: Rachel Maddow, California Rhodes Scholar, 1995." RhodesProject.com/scholar-contributions.

120 "That element of it is really hard": Jen Chung, "Rachel Maddow, Host of 'The Rachel Maddow Show,'" Gothamist.com, April 24, 2009.

120 "do things like eat and sleep and read my email": David Bauder, "Odd Couple: Rachel Maddow and Pat Buchanan," Associated Press, October 5, 2008.

121 "somebody else wrote for them": Interview, New York Film Academy, May 4, 2015.

121 "when I don't know what I'm talking about, it shows": Ibid.

121 "even if it is a really important story": Ibid.

122 "those things fall into place so that thing changes": Q&A Session, McCoy Family Center for Ethics in Society at Stanford University, March 16, 2013.

122 "I will never use them": Bob Ickes, "Maddow About You," *POZ*, June 2009.

123 "reporters and experts rather than analysts": Clara Jeffery, "Rachel Maddow's Star Power," *Mother Jones*, January/February 2009.

123 "independently corroborated by NBC News": "A Call to Earnest Citizenship: Rachel Maddow," *State of Belief*, April 22, 2017.

124 "Here's where they're not right'": "A Call to Earnest Citizenship: Rachel Maddow," *State of Belief*, April 22, 2017.

124 "'They're so terrible, they got something wrong'": Ibid.

125 "'we are going to run this part of it'": Ted Johnson, "Maddow's Unique Style Spikes Ratings," *Variety*, March 6, 2009.

125 "feel like it was an uncivil experience": "Rachel Maddow: The *Fresh Air* Interview," NPR, March 27, 2012.

125 "whether being a pundit is a worthwhile thing to be": Sam Boyd, "Channel Changer," *American Prospect*, October 1, 2008.

125 "'I am not like those other guys'": Ted Johnson, "Maddow's Unique Style Spikes Ratings," *Variety*, March 6, 2009.

126 "and doing good interviews": Jen Chung, "Rachel Maddow, Host of 'The Rachel Maddow Show,'" Gothamist.com, April 24, 2009.

126 "burritos or pizza or s'mores": David Hochman, "*Playboy* Interview: Rachel Maddow Talks Hillary, Hate Mail & More in Our First Non-Nude Issue," *Playboy*, February 2016.

126 "you can't focus on what I'm saying": Rachel Maddow at the Steinbeck Center, February 25, 2012.

126 "and I still am, to a certain extent": Matea Gold, "MSNBC's New Liberal Spark Plug," *Los Angeles Times*, September 29, 2008.

127 "is an active value for me": Howard Kurtz, "Rachel Maddow, MS-NBC's Newest Left Hand," *Washington Post*, Wednesday, August 27, 2008.

127 "It looks like they've got spangles on them": Clara Jeffery, "Rachel Maddow's Star Power," *Mother Jones*, January/February 2009.

127 "I am dressed up like an assistant principal": Edward Levine, "A Pundit in the Country," *New York Times*, October 17, 2008.

128 "at two in the morning": David Hinckley, "Maddow Rechannels Energy at Air America." *New York Daily News*, February 3, 2009.

128 "in an hour of television every single day": Jen Chung, "Rachel Maddow, Host of 'The Rachel Maddow Show,'" Gothamist.com, April 24, 2009.

128 "I could have a more private life": Terry Gross, "Rachel Maddow: The *Fresh Air* Interview," NPR, March 27, 2012.

128 "Does it make me a lesbian if I have a crush on you?": Amy Argetsinger, Roxanne Roberts, "Introducing Cable News's Latest Hotties," *Washington Post*, February 11, 2008.

128 "[but I] appreciate that people are kind": Joe Garofoli, "Maddow Annoyed by Dems, Flattered by Groupies," *San Francisco Chronicle*, March 28, 2009.

129 "I am a product": Rachel Maddow at the Steinbeck Center, February 25, 2012.

129 "no one would know who I was": Catie Lazarus, "Rachel Maddow," *Employee of the Month*, January 16, 2013.

129 "It shapes the character of the personal attacks": Colleen M. Lee, "The Inside Story from Rachel Maddow," *Curve*, October 9, 2008.

129 "that makes them want to kill me": Chloe Angyal, "The Feministing Five: Rachel Maddow," *Feministing*, October 23, 2010.

129 "snowfall disproves global warming": Transcript, *The Rachel Maddow Show*, February 16, 2010.

130 "I don't open my own mail": Louise France, "I'm Not a TV Anchor Babe. I'm a Big Lesbian Who Looks Like a Man," *The Guardian*, February 7, 2009.

130 "If you look out that window, you'll see snipers": David Hochman, "*Playboy* Interview: Rachel Maddow Talks Hillary, Hate Mail & More in Our First Non-Nude Issue," *Playboy*, February 2016.

130 "Now I think we accept different sources of authority": Terry

Gross, "Rachel Maddow: The *Fresh Air* Interview," NPR, March 27, 2012.

130 "feminism versus the world": Chloe Angyal, "The Feministing Five: Rachel Maddow," *Feministing*, October 23, 2010.

131 "I have bad time-management skills": Marisa Guthrie, "Rachel Maddow: How This Wonky-Tonk Woman Won TV," *Hollywood Reporter*, October 5, 2011.

131 "I am inured to it": Ted Johnson, "Maddow's Unique Style Spikes Ratings," *Variety*, March 6, 2009.

131 "out of fashion in Washington": Scott Pierce, "MSNBC's Maddow Thrives," *Deseret News*, February 26, 2009.

131 "I like wonky in a politician": Louise France, "I'm Not a TV Anchor Babe. I'm a Big Lesbian Who Looks Like a Man," *The Guardian*, February 7, 2009.

132 "and not feel terrible in the morning": David Hochman, *"Playboy* Interview: Rachel Maddow Talks Hillary, Hate Mail & More in Our First Non-Nude Issue," *Playboy*, February 2016.

Chapter 10: *Off the Clock*

133 "I go to great lengths to turn the brain off": Margaret Heilbrun, "Q&A: Rachel Maddow, Author of *Drift*," *Library Journal*, March 20, 2012.

133 "who is patient enough to put up with me": David Hochman, *"Playboy* Interview: Rachel Maddow Talks Hillary, Hate Mail & More in Our First Non-Nude Issue," *Playboy*, February 2016.

134 "Susan is more lovable than I am": Catie Lazarus, "Rachel Maddow," *Employee of the Month*, January 16, 2013.

134 "her mom has Fox News on all day": Ibid.

134 "We just treat it as received gospel": *The Ezra Klein Show*, February 9, 2016.

135 "we would neuter him as soon as he starts humping": Ibid.

135 "try to figure out why things happen": Ibid.

135 "I'd rush in and save them": Clara Jeffery, "Rachel Maddow's Star Power," *Mother Jones*, January/February 2009.

135 "you can do a lot of trashy thrillers": Ibid.

136 "It's cathartic for me": Benjamin Bell, "Maddow's a Softie for Sox' Pedroia," *Boston Herald*, November 9, 2009.

136 "I like making drinks even more than I like drinking them": "Q&A with Rachel Maddow," *Imbibe*, January 16, 2010.

136 "If not, I'm not": Clara Jeffery, "Rachel Maddow's Star Power," *Mother Jones*, January/February 2009.

136 "people who are waiting for me to produce a cocktail": Catie Lazarus, "Rachel Maddow," *Employee of the Month*, January 16, 2013.

137 "I don't believe in having cocktails without alcohol": Anna Fifield, "Dinner with the FT: Rachel Maddow," *Financial Times*, December 17, 2010.

137 "you should drink well": Rachel Maddow at the Steinbeck Center, February 25, 2012.

137 "I make tiny glasses of very big drinks": Clara Jeffery, "Rachel Maddow's Star Power," *Mother Jones*, January/February 2009.

137 "you probably shouldn't be drinking it": Ibid.

137 "or simple syrup for making cocktails and stuff": Rachel Maddow at the Steinbeck Center, February 25, 2012.

138 "neither of us has had a TV in years and years": T. Cole Rachel, "Interview with Rachel Maddow," *Dossier*, April 2009.

138 "what other people are doing": "A Call to Earnest Citizenship: Rachel Maddow," *State of Belief*, April 22, 2017.

138 "I'll just get sucked into it": "The *Out* 100: The Men & Women Who Made 2008," *Out*, November 2, 2008.

138 "The best thing in my life is my relationship": *The Howard Stern Show*, May 24, 2017.

139 "[to a place] that's not loud": Ibid.

139 "when we gain those marriage rights, I'm ambivalent": Shauna Swartz, "Radio Star Rachel Maddow," AfterEllen.com, January 29, 2007.

139 "and that's sad to me": David Hochman, "*Playboy* Interview: Rachel Maddow Talks Hillary, Hate Mail & More in Our First Non-Nude Issue," *Playboy*, February 2016.

139 "But I don't ever want it to make us normal": "The *Out* 100: The Men & Women Who Made 2008," *Out*, November 2, 2008.

139 "And I *like* gay culture": Marisa Guthrie, "Rachel Maddow: How This Wonky-Tonk Woman Won TV," *Hollywood Reporter*, October 5, 2011.

140 "Kids are coming out on Facebook now": David Hochman, "*Playboy* Interview: Rachel Maddow Talks Hillary, Hate Mail & More in Our First Non-Nude Issue," *Playboy*, February 2016.

140 "they damn well better have the right to": Mette Bach, "Air America's Sweetheart," *The Advocate*, June 19, 2008.

140 "for what you think is rightfully yours": "The *Out* 100: The Men & Women Who Made 2008," *Out*, November 2, 2008.

140 "can't do anything else and have to go home": Ibid.

141 "you shouldn't have to keep track of": Catie Lazarus, "Rachel Maddow," *Employee of the Month*, January 16, 2013.

141 "and that is no fun": Q&A Session, McCoy Family Center for Ethics in Society at Stanford University, March 16, 2013.

141 "how it was once they came out": Catie Lazarus, "Rachel Maddow," *Employee of the Month*, January 16, 2013.

141 "Everybody needs to find their own way": David Hochman, "*Playboy* Interview: Rachel Maddow Talks Hillary, Hate Mail & More in Our First Non-Nude Issue," *Playboy*, February 2016.

141 "when really we're just nervous": Catie Lazarus, "Rachel Maddow," *Employee of the Month*, January 16, 2013.

141 "by telling you what you've just told them": *Late Night with Conan O'Brien*, NBC, November 21, 2008.

142 "It's one way gay people need to stand up for ourselves": Clara Jeffery, "Rachel Maddow's Star Power," *Mother Jones*, January/February 2009.

142 "the moral arc of the universe bends toward justice": David Hochman, "*Playboy* Interview: Rachel Maddow Talks Hillary, Hate Mail & More in Our First Non-Nude Issue," *Playboy*, February 2016.

142 "the universe will kick your ass": Q&A Session, McCoy Family Center for Ethics in Society at Stanford University, March 16, 2013.

143 "than it does about being gay": Terry Gross, "Rachel Maddow: The *Fresh Air* Interview," NPR, March 27, 2012.

143 "and so I do not deserve her": Colleen M. Lee, "The Inside Story from Rachel Maddow," *Curve*, October 9, 2008.

143 "That rotates, but I am luck oriented": Edward Levine, "A Pundit in the Country," *New York Times*, October 17, 2008.

144 "It's about the fable you want to write about your own life": Julia Baird, "Rachel Maddow Comes Out on Top," *Newsweek*, November 21, 2008.

144 "and wonderful about these places": Heather Cassell, "American Fringe," *Bay Area Reporter*, February 25, 2010.

144 "I discovered old Polaroid cameras and peel-apart film": Loren King, "Pinhole Orientation: Mikula's Dream-Like Abstracts Are Meant to Be Unsettling," *Provincetown Banner*, October 22, 2009.

145 "the poignancy that makes them so beautiful to me": Jamie Wetherbe, "Refined Beauty: Artist Susan Mikula on Finding Beauty in Industry, Exclusive." *Pride*, February 23, 2010.

145 "but there's the downside to them, too": John Mitchell, "Capturing the Ghosts of Industry," *North Adams Transcript*, June 18, 2010.

146 "America's complete love affair with the instantaneous": Heather Cassell, "American Fringe," *Bay Area Reporter*, February 25, 2010.

146 "photography was made available to ordinary people": Cheryl Mazak, "Art and Artifact," *Curve*, March 2010.

146 "her day can be severely curtailed": Christopher Bonanos, "The Last Polaroid Artist?," susanmikula.com, 2013.

146 "It's like squeezing the color out of a sponge": Jessica Zack, "Susan Mikula, 'Master at the Sucker Punch,' at Lawson Gallery," *San Francisco Chronicle*, June 17, 2015.

147 "It's a crazy plan to go backward in time, not forward!": "Susan Mikula: Art, Inspiration and Heart," GoGetYourGirlOn.com, February 19, 2010.

147 "I'm so proud of her": "Big Shot," *Boston Globe*, December 27, 2008.

147 "It's the single clearest thing in my life": Julia Baird, "Rachel Maddow Comes Out on Top," *Newsweek*, November 21, 2008.

Chapter 11: *Behind the Scenes*

149 "and the show's only ninety percent done": Terry Gross, "Rachel Maddow: The *Fresh Air* Interview," NPR, March 27, 2012.

150 "This is going to happen no matter what I do": David Hochman, "*Playboy* Interview: Rachel Maddow Talks Hillary, Hate Mail & More in Our First Non-Nude Issue," *Playboy*, February 2016.

150 "it takes a village every night to get it on the air": Mark Joyella, "MSNBC's Rachel Maddow Hits No. 1 with Long, Complicated Segments Viewers Love," *Forbes*, December 31, 2018.

150 "Rachel is a one-woman data-mining operation": Matthew Gilbert, "Nude Cycling? That's Funny!," *Boston Globe*, June 19, 2009.

151 "And that is very rarely something overt": Ben Wallace-Wells, "Rachel Maddow's Quiet War." *Rolling Stone*, June 27, 2012.

151 "Before noon, all I'm capable of is marmalade and mumbling": Stephanie Palumbo, "How Rachel Maddow Lives Her Best Life," *O, The Oprah Magazine*, March 2012.

151 "by the time I get to work": Jen Chung, "Rachel Maddow, Host of 'The Rachel Maddow Show,'" Gothamist.com, April 24, 2009.

152 "I make this big grid which is very embarrassing": Jen Chung, "Rachel Maddow, Host of 'The Rachel Maddow Show,'" Gothamist.com, April 24, 2009.

152 "am a paper monster": Margaret Heilbrun, "Q&A: Rachel Maddow, Author of *Drift*," *Library Journal*, March 20, 2012.

153 "and we can introduce [it]": *The Ezra Klein Show*, February 9, 2016.

153 "I trust who blog on voting rights": Ibid.

153 "Nebraska has a unicameral legislature": Interview, New York Film Academy, May 4, 2015.

153 "I'd rather be my own thing": *The Ezra Klein Show*, February 9, 2016.

153 "as little of other people's analysis as I can": Sam Boyd, "Channel Changer," *American Prospect*, September 18, 2008.

154 "The best part of the story might be a very small detail": Interview, New York Film Academy, May 4, 2015.

154 "the better the storytelling has to be": Ibid.

154 "But you have to be good at it": Brian Steinberg, "As MSNBC Makes Changes, Rachel Maddow Presses On," *Variety*, February 1, 2016.

154 "which makes for a high-stress atmosphere": Katie Couric, "Rachel Maddow Tells Katie Couric, 'I'm Not Competing on the Pretty-Girl-on-Cable Front,'" *Glamour*, May 1, 2011.

155 "but we work it out": Jen Chung, "Rachel Maddow, Host of 'The Rachel Maddow Show,'" Gothamist.com, April 24, 2009.

156 "my level of confidence in the segments": Howard Kurtz, "Rachel Maddow Seizes Her Moment at Post–Keith Olbermann MSNBC," *Daily Beast*, February 27, 2011.

156 "It's a grumpy meeting. A little testy": Janet Malcolm, "Rachel Maddow: Trump's TV Nemesis," *New Yorker*, October 9, 2017.

156 "you can't spend that time covering something else": "A Call to Earnest Citizenship: Rachel Maddow," *State of Belief*, April 22, 2017.

156 "that's the thing that I know I would miss": Jen Chung, "Rachel Maddow, Host of 'The Rachel Maddow Show,'" Gothamist.com, April 24, 2009.

157 "'Between these two stories, what do you like?'": Interview, New York Film Academy, May 4, 2015.

157 "and doing what needs to be done": Terry Gross, "Rachel Maddow: The *Fresh Air* Interview," NPR, March 27, 2012.

157 "crushed under a pile of paper": Ben Wallace-Wells, "Rachel Maddow's Quiet War," *Rolling Stone*, June 27, 2012.

158 "based on what I said": Terry Gross, "Rachel Maddow: The *Fresh Air* Interview," NPR, March 27, 2012.

158 "so we start working on maps early": Ibid.

158 "or sometimes me dictating": Ibid.

158 "I don't start writing until six thirty": Janet Malcolm, "Rachel Maddow: Trump's TV Nemesis," *New Yorker*, October 9, 2017.

158 "the lives of all the people who work with me": Ibid.

159 "I give them eight minutes to make me up": *The Howard Stern Show*, May 24, 2017.

159 "But it works": Interview, New York Film Academy, May 4, 2015.

160 "and apologies for unbooking them": Interview, New York Film Academy, May 4, 2015.

160 "and she's going to ask hard questions": Brian Steinberg, "Inside Rachel Maddow's Plan to Reinvent Her MSNBC Show in Trump Era," *Variety*, January 17, 2017.

160 "It's unfortunate, but it happens": Interview, New York Film Academy, May 4, 2015.

160 "I'm completely mystified by [it]": Jen Chung, "Rachel Maddow, Host of 'The Rachel Maddow Show,'" Gothamist.com, April 24, 2009.

161 "no one can see me when I do the show": Ted Johnson, "Maddow's Unique Style Spikes Ratings," *Variety*, March 6, 2009.

161 "you're trying to move the world in a specific way": Interview, New York Film Academy, May 4, 2015.

162 "I can hear in her voice how serious it is": Ibid.

162 "and emailed the producer the video code": "Trinity College Students Reflect on Summer Television Internships at 30 Rock," Trinity College News Service, October 5, 2016.

163 "and have a voice that people can listen to": Interview, New York Film Academy, May 4, 2015.

163 "That stuff is gold": David Hochman, "*Playboy* Interview: Rachel Maddow Talks Hillary, Hate Mail & More in Our First Non-Nude Issue," *Playboy*, February 2016.

164 "as much fun as it would be to do": Matthew Gilbert, "Nude Cycling? That's Funny!," *Boston Globe*, June 19, 2009.

164 "don't sound authoritative": Interview, New York Film Academy, May 4, 2015.

164 "I can never, ever use them on camera": Ibid.

165 "but I don't tell people how I feel": Ibid.

165 "I have to kind of show myself a little bit": Ibid.

165 "and I fail at it constantly": Ben Wallace-Wells, "Rachel Maddow's Quiet War," *Rolling Stone*, June 27, 2012.

166 "My freedom": Ibid.

166 "I feel like it might weird me out": Catie Lazarus, "Rachel Maddow," *Employee of the Month*, January 16, 2013.

166 "It's a great compliment": Catie Lazarus, "Rachel Maddow," *Employee of the Month*, January 16, 2013.

167 "an inch at a time": Terry Gross, "Rachel Maddow: The *Fresh Air* Interview," NPR, March 27, 2012.

167 "week after week after week": Interview, New York Film Academy, May 4, 2015.

167 "It's hard to keep people for the long haul": Ben Wallace-Wells, "Rachel Maddow's Quiet War," *Rolling Stone*, June 27, 2012.

167 "I work very long, plodding days": Jen Chung, "Rachel Maddow, Host of 'The Rachel Maddow Show,'" Gothamist.com, April 24, 2009.

168 "and not reading my emails": Steve Krakauer, "So What Do You Do, MSNBC Host Rachel Maddow?," mediabistro, May 6, 2009.

168 "I'll have some more time [to do other things]": Jen Chung, "Rachel Maddow, Host of 'The Rachel Maddow Show,'" Gothamist.com, April 24, 2009.

Chapter 12: *Branching Out*

170 "which is ask people to do nothing": Matt Pressman, "Whatever Happened to Air America?," *Vanity Fair*, March 2009.

170 "who have gone on to a lot of other gigs": Tom Sturm, "Wonk and Circumstance," *Valley Advocate*, May 6, 2010.

170 "an appetite for really smart discussion of the news": Sasha Issenberg, "A Liberal Pundit Soars to a Prominent Perch," *Boston Globe*, September 8, 2008.

171 "more unpredictable": Chuck Barney, "Barney: Rachel Maddow Continues to Thrive at MSNBC," *San Jose Mercury News*, August 3, 2011.

171 "in the racket that is cable news": "The 75 Best People in the World," *Esquire*, October 2009.

171 "I'm trying to cover them": "Power Women," Forbes.com, 2010.

172 "talking about how I got here": Suzan Colon, "The New American Classic," *The Advocate*, December 2, 2008.

172 "to help people come to their own conclusions": Katie Couric, "Rachel Maddow Tells Katie Couric, 'I'm Not Competing on the Pretty-Girl-on-Cable Front,'" *Glamour*, May 1, 2011.

172 "I'm protecting what I'm doing more": Winnie McCroy, "The Queer Issue: A Conversation with Rachel Maddow, Reluctant Sex Symbol," *Village Voice*, June 24, 2009.

172 "the answer is no": Marisa Guthrie, "Rachel Maddow: How This Wonky-Tonk Woman Won TV," *Hollywood Reporter*, October 5, 2011.

173 "I'll do anything for George Clooney": Ibid.

173 "that the Kardashians don't have jobs": David Hochman, "*Playboy* Interview: Rachel Maddow Talks Hillary, Hate Mail & More in Our First Non-Nude Issue," *Playboy*, February 2016.

174 "what's happening on TV at that moment": Winnie McCroy, "The Queer Issue: A Conversation with Rachel Maddow, Reluctant Sex Symbol," *Village Voice*, June 24, 2009.

174 "men and women, gay and straight, find very appealing": Ibid.

174 "there's a real sense of play in what she does": Ibid.

174 "who is fashionable seems gay to me": *The Howard Stern Show*, May 24, 2017.

174 "as the other guys on MSNBC": Winnie McCroy, "The Queer Issue: A Conversation with Rachel Maddow, Reluctant Sex Symbol," *Village Voice*, June 24, 2009.

175 "it's business upstairs, party downstairs": "Rachel Maddow, Storyteller and Gun Lover," CBS News, May 15, 2016.

175 "Guess what? I don't want to": *Watch What Happens: Live*, May 1, 2013.

176 "My main concern is keeping the quality of the show high": Yvonne Villarreal, "Obama Won, Now What Does Maddow's Future Hold?" *Los Angeles Times*, April 22, 2009.

176 "that they're going to show me up on my own program": Rachel Maddow at the Steinbeck Center, February 25, 2012.

177 "as a socialist": Colleen M. Lee, "The Inside Story from Rachel Maddow," *Curve*, October 9, 2008.

177 "the opportunity to interview her": Ali Frick, "Maddow Fails to Question Huckabee on His Recent Anti-Gay Statements; Update: Maddow Responds," ThinkProgress.org, November 21, 2008.

177 "over his ugly evangelical conservatism": Michelangelo Signorile. "Whither Maddow?," *The Advocate*, February 1, 2009.

178 "I don't have that option": Howard Kurtz, "Maddow, on a Military Mission," *Washington Post*, February 15, 2010.

178 "they get to talk without being interrupted": Bob Ickes, "Maddow About You," *POZ*, June 2009.

179 "a responsibility to pay that back": Terry Gross, "The *Fresh Air* Interview," NPR, March 27, 2012.

179 "It just sounds like no fun": Janet Malcolm, "Rachel Maddow: Trump's TV Nemesis," *New Yorker*, October 9, 2017.

179 "closing off from the world": Kara Mayer Robinson, "10 Questions with Journalist Rachel Maddow," WebMD.com, August 19, 2016.

179 "I lose my will and my ability to focus": Ben Wallace-Wells, "Rachel Maddow's Quiet War," *Rolling Stone*, June 27, 2012.

179 "and it can be alienating": David Hochman, *"Playboy* Interview: Rachel Maddow Talks Hillary, Hate Mail & More in Our First Non-Nude Issue," *Playboy*, February 2016.

179 "I don't know what it is": "Rachel Maddow, Storyteller and Gun Lover," CBS News, May 15, 2016.

179 "to stop my life": Kara Mayer Robinson, "10 Questions with Journalist Rachel Maddow," WebMD.com, August 19, 2016.

179 "but right now I don't": David Hochman, *"Playboy* Interview: Rachel Maddow Talks Hillary, Hate Mail & More in Our First Non-Nude Issue," *Playboy*, February 2016.

180 "But Maddow totally reads the book": Marisa Guthrie, "Rachel Maddow: How This Wonky-Tonk Woman Won TV," *Hollywood Reporter*, October 5, 2011.

181 "some of the best reporting I've ever done in my life": Interview, New York Film Academy, May 4, 2015.

181 "where it is that you are": Alex Weprin, "Rachel Maddow Speaks Out About Afghanistan Trip." *TV Newser*, July 5, 2010.

182 "so it's about birds and oil and Baghdad": Catie Lazarus, "Rachel Maddow," *Employee of the Month*, January 16, 2013.

183 "anything this cool ever again in my life": Catherine Taibi, "Rachel Maddow Reveals 'Simpsons' Cameo," *Huffington Post*, November 1, 2013.

183 "I'm not trying to pick up extra work": Andrea Morabito, "TCA:

MSNBC Inks New Deal with Rachel Maddow," *Broadcasting & Cable*, August 2, 2011.

183 "It's just not true. Honestly. I swear": Ad, *Boston Globe*, March 26, 2010.

184 "most of the people who do it are scoundrels": Interview, New York Film Academy, May 4, 2015.

184 "so you ought to be worth knowing": Terry Gross, "Rachel Maddow: The *Fresh Air* Interview," NPR, March 27, 2012.

185 "I hope they die in a fire": Diana Scholl, "Rachel Maddow: 'Glenn Beck Was My Favorite Person of All Time on Radio,'" *New York*, September 2, 2010.

186 "Rachel is our quarterback": Kelefa Sanneh, "Twenty-Four-Hour Party People," *New Yorker*, September 2, 2013.

186 "Someday I'm going to do the show I want to do": Marisa Guthrie, "Rachel Maddow: How This Wonky-Tonk Woman Won TV," *Holly-wood Reporter*, October 5, 2011.

187 "it's more of a long-form idea": Terry Gross, "Rachel Maddow: The *Fresh Air* Interview," NPR, March 27, 2012.

187 "it's supposed to be hard for us to go to war": Rachel Maddow at the Steinbeck Center, February 25, 2012.

188 "and that was always inculcated in me": Terry Gross, "Rachel Maddow: The *Fresh Air* Interview," NPR, March 27, 2012.

188 "war is always the single, worst option": Aaron Sekhri, "Rachel Maddow Visits Stanford for First Time Since Graduating," *Stanford Daily*, March 16, 2013.

188 "a sharply argued commentary that many conservatives could buy into": David Horsey, "Rachel Maddow Plots America's 'Drift' to Easy War," *Los Angeles Times*, April 16, 2012.

189 "that is both unfair and unsustainable": Q&A Session, McCoy Family Center for Ethics in Society at Stanford University, March 16, 2013.

189 "for an America at war that doesn't feel it": Ibid.

189 "kids in the Model UN than you think": Ben Wallace-Wells, "Rachel Maddow's Quiet War," *Rolling Stone*, June 27, 2012.

189 "'Do more "Moment of Geek"—my kid loves it!'": Ibid.

189 "A French 75": Sarah Watson, "A Conversation with Rachel Maddow," Popmatters.com, April 26, 2012.

Chapter 13: *Settling In*

192   "of ways you can create an audience": Lucas Shaw, "New MSNBC Host Chris Hayes Channels Rachel Maddow—and Tim Robbins," Reuters, August 1, 2011.

192   "I would look dumb": Howard Kurtz, "Rachel Maddow Seizes Her Moment at Post–Keith Olbermann MSNBC," *Daily Beast*, February 27, 2011.

192   "to create kind of a neutral visual experience": Terry Gross, "Rachel Maddow: The *Fresh Air* Interview," NPR, March 27, 2012.

192–93   "it's because I believe they are worth hearing": Erik Wemple, "Rachel Maddow: 'I Don't Necessarily Want to Hear from the White House on Almost Anything,'" *Washington Post*, April 6, 2017.

193   "or I wish you didn't exist": Ibid.

193   "so I'm always a little reluctant": "The *Out* 100: The Men & Women Who Made 2008," *Out*, November 2, 2008.

193   "rather than getting something out of them": *Washington Journal*, August 21, 2007.

193   *"Oh, please let me interview you"*: Rachel Maddow, *Drift* (New York: Random House, 2012).

194   "not the stuff of record": Anna Fifield, "Dinner with the FT: Rachel Maddow," *Financial Times*, December 17, 2010.

194   "Dick Cheney gets far too much credit than he deserves": Robert Nesti, "Reality Check with Rachel Maddow," *The Edge*, July 27, 2006.

194   "Ann Coulter would not meet that requirement": David Hochman, "*Playboy* Interview: Rachel Maddow Talks Hillary, Hate Mail & More in Our First Non-Nude Issue," *Playboy*, February 2016.

194   "a really funny turkey noise that makes me happy every time": Leah Chernikoff, "Rachel Maddow Is MSNBC's Prime Time Star," *New York Daily News*, October 29, 2008.

195   "has locked up all the conservative audience": David Hochman, "*Playboy* Interview: Rachel Maddow Talks Hillary, Hate Mail & More in Our First Non-Nude Issue," *Playboy*, February 2016.

195   "I'd rather have none at all than a grain too much": Ben Wallace-Wells, "Rachel Maddow's Quiet War," *Rolling Stone*, June 27, 2012.

195 "it's weird to have dinner with people you cover": Rachel Maddow at the Steinbeck Center, February 25, 2012.

196 "it was attached to Sarah Palin": Ibid.

196 "calling a lie a lie, and a liar a liar": Transcript, *The Rachel Maddow Show*, October 13, 2008.

196 "'It's very nice to meet you'": Rachel Maddow at the Steinbeck Center, February 25, 2012.

197 "I'll think about it": Ibid.

197 "makes people focus on what's really important": Mark Joyella, "MSNBC's Rachel Maddow Hits No. 1 with Long, Complicated Segments Viewers Love," *Forbes*, December 31, 2018.

197 "maybe my adrenaline pump was just installed backward": Stephanie Palumbo, "How Rachel Maddow Lives Her Best Life," *O, The Oprah Magazine*, March 2012.

198 "and that's usually because I'm hungover": Clara Jeffery, "Rachel Maddow's Star Power," *Mother Jones*, January/February 2009.

198 "I let the dog look at the sheep": Edward Levine, "A Pundit in the Country," *New York Times*, October 17, 2008.

199 "like putting a hat on a horse": Wendy Goodman, "Where Rachel Maddow Is Allowed to Watch TV," *New York*, April 24, 2014.

199 "and watch football really loudly": Ibid.

199 "I'd bring Cuban rum—we both like that": Chloe Angyal, "The Feministing Five: Rachel Maddow," *Feministing*, October 23, 2010.

200 "we just keep to ourselves": "Rachel Maddow, Storyteller and Gun Lover," CBS News, May 15, 2016.

200 "since I laid eyes on her": Stephanie Palumbo, "How Rachel Maddow Lives Her Best Life," *O, The Oprah Magazine*, March 2012.

200 "It's not a stretch for me to incorporate that stuff": Christopher Lisotta, "Ready for Her Primetime Debut," *Broadcasting & Cable*, September 5, 2008.

200 "I'm a creature of the online world": Steve Krakauer, "So What Do You Do, MSNBC Host Rachel Maddow?," mediabistro, May 6, 2009.

201 "the people who are doing good work": Ibid.

201 "'understand the Republican world a little bit better'": Marisa Guthrie,

"Rachel Maddow: How This Wonky-Tonk Woman Won TV," *Hollywood Reporter*, October 5, 2011.

202 "It sucks you in!": Amy Smith, "Star Reporter," *Austin Chronicle*, March 8, 2013.

Chapter 14: *The 2016 Elections and What's Next for Rachel*

204 "just in terms of suspense": Brian Steinberg, "Brian Williams, Rachel Maddow Will Spearhead MSNBC Live Politics Coverage," *Variety*, January 25, 2016.

204 "people who care enough to have an opinion": Terry Gross, "Rachel Maddow: The *Fresh Air* Interview," NPR, March 27, 2012.

205 "You have to use a contraction": David Hochman, "*Playboy* Interview: Rachel Maddow Talks Hillary, Hate Mail & More in Our First Non-Nude Issue," *Playboy*, February 2016.

205 "watching clips of people talking about him": Brian Steinberg, "Brian Williams, Rachel Maddow Will Spearhead MSNBC Live Politics Coverage," *Variety*, January 25, 2016.

205 "than about the Republican Party": David Hochman, "*Playboy* Interview: Rachel Maddow Talks Hillary, Hate Mail & More in Our First Non-Nude Issue," *Playboy*, February 2016.

207 "in the rain with no wipers and no lights": Ben Wallace-Wells, "Rachel Maddow's Quiet War," *Rolling Stone*, June 27, 2012.

207 "the amount of useful information in the world": "A Call to Earnest Citizenship: Rachel Maddow," *State of Belief*, April 22, 2017.

207 "Our president-elect is lying to us": Brian Steinberg, "Rachel Maddow Quietly Tackles New Projects at MSNBC," *Variety*, November 16, 2018.

207 "about the fact that they're not true": "A Call to Earnest Citizenship: Rachel Maddow," *State of Belief*, April 22, 2017.

208 "in a very long time": "A Call to Earnest Citizenship: Rachel Maddow," *State of Belief*, April 22, 2017.

208 "there's a lot to explain": Brian Steinberg, "Rachel Maddow Quietly Tackles New Projects at MSNBC," *Variety*, November 16, 2018.

208 "someone sitting on a hot stove": Mathew Ingram, "Trump Tax Reveal: Major Scoop or Overhyped Nothingburger?," Fortune.com, March 16, 2017.

209 "exactly what it is we've got": Transcript, *The Rachel Maddow Show*, March 14, 2017.

210 "really psyched that we broke this story": Lloyd Grove, "'We Broke the Story Correctly': Rachel Maddow Returns Fire on Her Trump Tax Scoop," *The Daily Beast*, March 15, 2017.

210 "I did it right": Janet Malcolm, "Rachel Maddow: Trump's TV Nemesis," *New Yorker*, October 9, 2017.

210 "that stuff makes a lot of sense": Terry Gross, "Rachel Maddow: The *Fresh Air* Interview," NPR, March 27, 2012.

211 "I don't think that a gun would make me safer": *The Howard Stern Show*, May 24, 2017.

211 "disappear from the collective consciousness and public view": Matt Flegenheimer, "The Year the News Accelerated to Trump Speed," *New York Times*, December 29, 2017.

212 "you can't plan ahead, ever": Marisa Guthrie, "Rachel Maddow on Trump, Record Ratings, and a Possible Roger Ailes Meeting," *Hollywood Reporter*, April 13, 2017.

212 "whatever it is he's just said": Ben Wallace-Wells, "Rachel Maddow's Quiet War," *Rolling Stone*, June 27, 2012.

212 "in terms of trying to get factual information": "A Call to Earnest Citizenship: Rachel Maddow," *State of Belief*, April 22, 2017.

212 "just focus on what they *do*": Brian Flood, "Rachel Maddow on How She Doubled Viewership Under Trump: 'I Stopped Covering the Twitter Feed,'" TheWrap.com, March 3, 2017.

212 "as if they are a silent movie": Ibid.

213 "it requires the most original thought": "A Call to Earnest Citizenship: Rachel Maddow," *State of Belief*, April 22, 2017.

213 "to get stuff as soon as it happens": Q&A Session, McCoy Family Center for Ethics in Society at Stanford University, March 16, 2013.

213 "his first meeting with special counsel Robert Mueller": *The Rachel Maddow Show*, April 25, 2018.

214 "make you feel implicated by your silence": Transcript, *The Rachel Maddow Show*, June 30, 2017.

215 "But you know, I don't know": Erik Wemple, "Rachel Maddow: 'I Don't Necessarily Want to Hear from the White House on Almost Anything,'" *Washington Post*, April 6, 2017.

215 "something that is definitely not work": Janet Malcolm, "Rachel Maddow: Trump's TV Nemesis," *New Yorker*, October 9, 2017.

215 "you stop making sense and stop being creative": Ibid.

215 "I am very, very excited about it!": Michaylah Kimbler, "Rachel Maddow Gushes About Her New York Times Crossword," *The Advocate*, March 2, 2018.

216 "And that feels very un-American to me": Terry Gross, "Rachel Maddow: The *Fresh Air* Interview," NPR, March 27, 2012.

216 "the life and legacy of Spiro T. Agnew, I might apply": Brian Steinberg, "Rachel Maddow Quietly Tackles New Projects at MSNBC," *Variety*, November 16, 2018.

217 "a husk of my former self": Ibid.

217 "falling asleep in the Thanksgiving mashed potatoes": Transcript: "Rachel Celebrates 10 Years on the Air," *The Rachel Maddow Show*, September 7, 2018.

217 "ever in my whole career": Jessica Heslam, "Rachel Maddow Slams 'Creep' Scott Brown," *Boston Herald*, March 26, 2010.

218 "I don't ever, ever, ever wanna do it": Interview, New York Film Academy, May 4, 2015.

218 "who wanted me to, would, frankly": Dan Rosenblum, "Rachel Maddow Doesn't Want to Run for Office," *The Atlantic*, March 30, 2012.

218 "you just don't do it": David Hochman, "*Playboy* Interview: Rachel Maddow Talks Hillary, Hate Mail & More in Our First Non-Nude Issue," *Playboy*, February 2016.

218 "That's what keeps me in business": Ibid.

219 "that they don't want known": "A Call to Earnest Citizenship: Rachel Maddow," *State of Belief*, April 22, 2017.

219 "we'll be working as hard, if not harder": "Mark Joyella, "MSNBC's Rachel Maddow Hits No. 1 with Long, Complicated Segments Viewers Love," *Forbes*, December 31, 2018.

219 "five nights a week, fifty weeks a year": "A Call to Earnest Citizenship: Rachel Maddow," *State of Belief*, April 22, 2017.

219 "I have found something I am good at": Jessica Pressler, "The Dr. Maddow Show," *New York*, November 2, 2008.

INDEX